# APORIAS

MERIDIAN

*Crossing Aesthetics*

Werner Hamacher

& David E. Wellbery

*Editors*

Translated by
Thomas Dutoit

*Stanford*
*University*
*Press*

*Stanford*
*California*
*1993*

# APORIAS

---

DYING—
awaiting (one another at)
the "limits of truth"

MOURIR—
s'attendre aux "limites de
la vérité"

*Jacques Derrida*

Originally published in French in 1993
as "Apories: Mourir-s'attendre aux
limites de la vérité," in *Le Passage
des frontières: Autour du travail de
Jacques Derrida* by Editions Galilée.

© 1993 by Editions Galilée.

Stanford University Press
Stanford, California
© 1993 by the Board of Trustees of the
Leland Stanford Junior University

Printed in the United States of America

CIP data appear at the end of the book

Stanford University Press publications
are distributed exclusively by
Stanford University Press within
the United States, Canada, and Mexico;
they are distributed exclusively by
Cambridge University Press
throughout the rest of the world.

*In memory of Koitchi Toyosaki*

# Preamble

In advance, I thank you for your patience in what you are going to endure.

Dare I say that all this will be said (destined, addressed) to you as a way of thanking?

I have often denigrated thankfulness and the business of thanking [*les commerces du merci*]. I have doubted it too often—up to the point of publishing these doubts, quite recently. I have felt the ingratitude of expressing one's gratitude too often for me to dare say my thankfulness, or formulate a few sentences that could measure my gratitude here.

Twelve years ago, when I did not expect the opportunity of this present conference,* I had already sensed this disproportion and this impossibility. Like today, already then I did not know whom to thank first: our hosts at Cerisy, Edith Heurgon, Jean Ricardou, Maurice de Gandillac, Catherine de Gandillac, Philippe Kister, who first had the generous idea of this conference and who carried it out so well? Or the guests [*les hôtes*] of these hosts [*ces hôtes*] whom you are, all of you? Or, between these guests and those hosts, she to whom all of us without doubt owe our being here? Indeed, I

---

*The conference was entitled "Le Passage des frontières (autour de Jacques Derrida)." It took place at Cerisy-la-Salle, July 11–21, 1992. Derrida delivered his paper on July 15, 1992.—TRANS.

can testify to what Marie-Louise Mallet has done, ever since the first preparatory meetings where she thought out and projected this conference, along with Catherine Paoletti, Charles Alunni, and René Major. I can testify to it, as you can, too, and maybe a little better than you—allow me to retain this privilege. Even though you already know it, I can and I want to testify to the lucidity, generosity, and infinite patience with which, day after day, for almost two years, she has been the providence of this conference. I see no other word: she has been its pro-vidence with regard to what she has foreseen and projected, its providence with regard to what she has destined, given, and accorded—thereby according us to what she accorded to us—with the grace that is hers, her welcoming grace [ *grâce prévenante*], I would say, twisting a little Malebranche's expression. And, as one always does with her, I hear accord, a chord, as one says in music.

Allow me also to dedicate these preliminary reflections to the memory of Koitchi Toyosaki, an address that will not prevent me from addressing you. The other night we were reminded that in 1980 this great friend of mine was here. On a bench in the garden that I can almost see from here, I had a conversation with him, which was almost the last. (With him, as with other friends, despite or because of my admiration, I will have spoken so little, too little.) His father had just died, and Koitchi had to leave Cerisy abruptly. Before he did, on that very bench, he spoke of his father—his profession (law, I believe) and his illness. He had expected the death that caught him here by surprise.

# Contents

# APORIAS

DYING—
awaiting (one another at)
the "limits of truth"

MOURIR—
s'attendre aux "limites de
la vérité"

# § 1 Finis

"Limits of truth," with the prudence of quotation marks, is of course a citation. A concession to the times: today one would scarcely risk putting forth such a disquieting phrase without sheltering oneself behind some kind of paternity.[1] In this case, Diderot's authority will appear all the more reassuring since he seems to denounce a "general defect," in particular that of "letting oneself be carried beyond the limits of truth."

How can one cross the borders of truth? And what "defect" would this betray, what "general defect"?

Crossing this strange border and "letting oneself be carried *beyond* the limits of truth" must be possible, indeed inevitable, in order for such a *defect* to exceed the singular cases, and thereby spread its contagion to the point of becoming "general."

What does "beyond" mean in this case? By itself, the expression "limits of truth" can certainly be understood—and this would be an *indication*—as the fact that the truth is precisely limited, *finite*, and confined within its borders. In sum, the truth is not everything, one would then say, for there is more, something else or something better: truth is finite [*finie*]. Or worse: truth, it's finished [*c'est fini*]. However, by itself, the same expression can signify—and this time it would not be an indication but the *law* of a negative *prescription*—that the limits of truth are borders that must not be exceeded. In both these cases it remains that a certain border crossing does

I

not seem impossible as soon as truth is confined. As soon as truth is a limit or has limits, its own, and assuming that it knows some limits, as the expression goes, truth would be a certain relation to what terminates or determines it.

How would Diderot account for this passage beyond truth, a passage that is certainly illegitimate, but so often repeated or deadly, by defect, a "general defect"? Most of all, in what name does he sometimes ask to be *pardoned*? For, in a kind of challenge, Diderot asks to be pardoned. In sum, he provokes us to think what the pardon can be when it touches upon the limits of truth. Is it a pardon among others? And why, in this transgression of truth, would death be part of the game?

Diderot asks pardon for Seneca, more precisely for the author of *De brevitate vitae* (whose reading he is right to recommend, from the first word to the last, despite the brevity of life that will have been so short, in any case). In his *Essai sur la vie de Sénèque le philosophe*, Diderot pretends to contend with the philosopher. In truth, he points his accusing finger back toward himself, Diderot, and toward what he calls *autobiographico more*, "the story of my life." While pretending to accuse Seneca, for whom he apparently demands pardon, Diderot in truth asks pardon for himself, from the very moment that he also accuses himself in the name of Seneca. This is the story of my life—that is what must always be heard when someone speaks of someone else, cites or praises him or her:

> This defect of letting oneself be carried by the interest of the cause that one is defending beyond the limits of truth is such a general defect that Seneca must sometimes be pardoned for it.
>
> I did not read the third chapter [of *De brevitate vitae*] without blushing: it is the story of my life. Happy is he who does not depart convinced that he has lived only a very small part of his life!

Diderot thus implies, in a sigh, something that he does not confide in the open, as if he had to address such a universal complaint *in secret*. One could use the future anterior to translate the time of this murmuring: "Ah! how short life will have been!" Then he concludes:

This treatise is beautiful. I recommend its reading to all men, but above all to those who are inclined toward perfection in the fine arts. They will learn here how little they have worked, and that the mediocrity of all kinds of productions should be attributed just as often to the loss of time as to the lack of talent.

Now if, aroused by curiosity, we reread this chapter of *De la brièveté de la vie*, which made Diderot blush because he reflected in advance upon "the story of my life," what would we find? Well, we would discover that this discourse on death also contains, among so many other things, a *rhetoric of borders*, a lesson in wisdom concerning the lines that delimit the right of absolute property, the right of property to our own life, the proper of our existence, in sum, a treatise about the tracing of traits as the borderly edges of what in sum *belongs to us* [*nous revient*], belonging as much to us as we properly belong to it.

What about borders with respect to death? About borders of truth and borders of property? We are going to wander about in the neighborhood of this question.

Between Diderot and Seneca, what can, first of all, be at stake is knowing what the property of "my life" is, and who could be its "master"; it is also knowing whether *to give* is something other than *to waste*, that is, whether "to give one's life by sharing it" is in sum something other than "wasting one's time." Wasting one's time would amount to wasting the only good of which one has the *right* to be avaricious and jealous, the unique and property itself, the unique property that "one would take pride in guarding jealously." What is therefore in question is to think the very principle of jealousy as the primitive passion for property and as the concern for the proper, for the proper possibility, in question for everyone, of his existence. It is a matter of thinking the very and only thing to which one can testify. It is as if one could first be—or not be— jealous of oneself, jealous to the point of dying [*crever*]. Thus, according to Seneca, there would be a property, a right of property to one's own life. In sum, the border (*finis*) of this property would be more essential, more originary, and more proper than those of any other territory in the world. As Seneca says, one is never surprised enough by a certain "blindness of human intelligence" with respect to these borders (*fines*) and to these ends. Of what end (*finis*) does one mean to speak of here? And why does this end always arrive early? Prematurely? Immaturely?

1. Men do not suffer anyone to seize their estates, and if there is even the slightest dispute about the limit of their lands [*fines: si exigua contentio de modo finium:* it is indeed a question of tracing and negotiating (*traiter*) the limits, *de finibus*], they rush to stones and arms; yet, they let others trespass upon their own life [*in vitam suam*]— nay, they themselves even lead in those [*ipsi etiam*] who will eventually possess it. No one is to be found who is willing to share his money, yet to how many does each one of us give one's life by sharing it! In guarding their fortune [*in continendo patrimonio*] men are often close-fisted, yet, when it comes to the matter of wasting time, they show themselves most prodigal of the only thing that one would take pride in guarding jealously [as another French translation puts it, and as the English translation by Basore also puts it, "the case of the one thing in which it is right to be miserly": *in eo cujus unius honesta avaritia est*].

2. And so I should like to lay hold upon someone from the company of older men and say: "I see that you have reached the farthest limit of human life [*ad ultimum aetatis humanae*], you are pressing hard upon your hundredth year, or are even beyond it. Come now, recall your life . . . , look back in memory and consider . . . how little of yourself was left to you: you will perceive that you are dying before your season [*quam exiguum tibi de tuo relictum sit: intelleges te immaturum mori*].[2]

This exhortation is addressed to a centenary, and virtually to anyone who finds himself at a major turning point in life, a day of some fearsome birthday. But after having wondered, in sum, why man—and not the animal—always dies before his time, while also understanding that he dies *immaturus,* immaturely and prematurely, Seneca describes the absolute imminence, the imminence of death at every instant. This imminence of a disappearance that is by essence premature seals the union of the possible and the impossible, of fear and desire, and of mortality and immortality, in being-to-death.

What does he conclude from this? That to put off until later, to defer (*differre*), and above all to defer wisdom, wise resolutions, is to deny one's condition as mortal. One then gives in to forgetting and to distraction; one dissimulates to oneself being-to-death:

> You live as if you were destined to live forever, no thought of your frailty ever enters your head, of how much time has already gone by you take no heed. You squander time as if you drew from a full and abundant supply, so all the while that day which you bestow on some person or thing is perhaps your last. You have all the fears of mortals and all the desires of immortals. . . . What foolish forgetfulness of mortality [*Quae tam stulta mortalitatis oblivio*] to defer [*differre*] wise resolutions [*sana consilia*] to the fiftieth or sixtieth year, and to intend to begin life at a point to which few have attained.[3]

What should be understood here *by the end*?

In his *De finibus*, Cicero is, as always, attentive to the crossing of borders between languages, Greek and Latin.[4] He is careful to justify his translations, whose stakes he no doubt assesses. That is not all. What does the author of *Libellus de optima genera oratorum* also do, he who was one of the first to give advice to translators (notably to avoid the literality of *verbum pro verbo*)? He goes so far as to worry about crossing the borders of language, thereby increasing his own anxiety about the translation of the word for *border*, precisely. He explains what he translates *by the end*:

> Sentis enim, credo, me iam diu, quod *telos* Graeci dicunt, id dicere tum extremum, tum ultimum, tum summum; licebit etiam *finem* pro extremo aut ultimo dicere: You see, I believe, what the Greeks call *telos*; for a long time already I have called it at times the extreme, at times the ultimate, and at other times the supreme; instead of extreme or ultimate, one can even call it *end* (3:26; my emphasis).

In order to begin, again, even before an introduction, *by the end*—since we are convoked to the crossing of borders *by the end*, that is, by the ends or confines (*finis* is therefore the term, the edge, the limit, the border, most often that of a territory and of a country)—let us suppose that I now have a few sentences at my disposal. They can be *negative*, *affirmative*, or *interrogative*. Let us suppose that, while having these sentences at my disposal, I dispose them *among us.* Among us so as to *share* them. To share them with you, as a common good or a number shared in confidence, in sum, a password. Or else to share and unshare them among themselves; or, finally, in order that they, in turn, share us and perhaps separate us.

Let us consider, for example, this negative sentence: "death *has no* border." Or else, let us consider one of these affirmations, which all imply something completely different: "death *is* a border," "according to an almost universal figure, death is represented as the crossing of a border, a voyage between the here and the beyond, with or without a ferryman, with or without a barge, with or without elevation, toward this or that place beyond the grave." Here, now, is an interrogation: "Can death be reduced to some line crossing, to a departure, to a separation, to a step, and therefore to a *decease?*" And, finally, here is a proposition that could be called interro-denegative: "Is not death, like decease, the crossing of a border, that is, a trespassing on death [*un trépas*], an overstepping or a transgression (*transire*, "*sic transit*," etc.)?"

You have noticed that all these propositions, whatever their modality, involve a certain *pas* [step, not].

*Il y va d'un certain pas.* [It involves a certain step/not; he goes along at a certain pace.]

Does not this very sentence itself, *il y va d'un certain pas,* belong to the French language? Both effectively and legitimately? Belonging to the French language, it would also testify to that language. *Il y va d'un certain pas:* indeed, this speaks for itself. What can it mean?

First, perhaps, that this *incipit, il y va d'un certain pas*—which could just as well immobilize itself like a monument and fix the "here lies" of a word, the *pas* of a recumbent corpse—is not only a part of the *body* of the French language, a member, an object or a subject, something or someone that would belong to the French language as a part belongs to a whole, an element in a class or in an ensemble. Insofar as it speaks, this sentence—*il y va d'un certain pas—would* also *testify* to its belonging. The event of this *attestation* would testify not only to the enigma of what *testifying* means, that is, to the fact that the testimony of belonging does not simply belong to the *ensemble* of which it testifies, but also, consequently, that belonging to a language is undoubtedly not comparable to any other mode of inclusion: for example, to limit ourselves to a few elements, belonging to a language does not compare, at first sight, with *inclusion* in the space of citizenship or nationality; natural, historical, or political borders; geography or geo-politics; soil, blood, or social class. As soon as these totalities are overdetermined, or rather contaminated, by the events of language (let us say instead, by the events of the mark), which they all just as necessarily imply, they, in turn, are no longer thoroughly what they are or what one thinks they are, that is, they are no longer identical to themselves, hence no longer simply identifiable and to that extent no longer determinable. Such totalities therefore no longer authorize simple inclusions of a part in the whole. For this *pas* involves the line that terminates all determination, the final or definitional line—*peras* this time rather than *telos*. And *peras* is precisely what Cicero could also have translated by *finis*. The Greek word *peras*—term (here, a synonym of the Greek word *terma*), end or limit, extremity—puts us also on the path of *peran*, which means "beyond," on the other side, and even vis-à-vis. It also puts us on the path of *peraō*: I penetrate (Aeschylus, for example, says: *peraō* a place or a country, *eis khôran*), I traverse by penetrating, I cross through, I cross over life's term, *terma tou biou*, for example. Recall the very last words, indeed the ending, of Sophocles' *Oedipus the King*. At that point the chorus addresses the people, the inhabitants of the country, the *enoikoi*, those who live at the heart of the fatherland (*O patras Thebes enoikoi*). Speaking of Oedipus' last day, before his death [*trépas*], the chorus tells them at the end of the story: "Look upon that last day always [*ten teleutaian emeran*]. Count no mortal happy [*olbizein*] till he has passed the final limit of his life [*prin an terma tou biou perasei*] secure from pain [*meden algeinon pathōn*]."[5] I cannot consider myself happy, or even believe myself to have been happy, before having crossed, passed, and surpassed the last instant of my own life, even if up to that point I have been happy in a life that will have been, in any case, so short. What, then, is it to cross the ultimate border? What is it to pass the term of one's life (*terma tou biou*)? Is it possible? Who has ever done it and who can testify to it? The "I enter," crossing the threshold, this "I pass" (*peraō*) puts us on the path, if I may say, of the *aporos* or of the *aporia*: the difficult or the impracticable, here the impossible, passage, the refused, denied, or prohibited passage, indeed the nonpassage, which can in fact be something else, the event of a coming or of a future advent [*événement de venue ou d'avenir*], which no longer has the form of the movement that consists in passing, traversing, or transiting. It would be the "coming to pass" of an event that would no longer have the form or the appearance of a *pas*: in sum, a coming without *pas*.

*Il y va d'un certain pas*: all these words and each of these enunciations would therefore belong, hypothetically and on account of this clause of nonbelonging that we have just noted, to the French language. Legitimately and effectively, such a sentence testifies to this belonging; it says in French: that's French. Just as it should be.

At Cerisy-la-Salle what is said *just as it should be* belongs to the French language. Here it is necessary to speak French. French makes the law. And since this law should also be a law of hospitality—the *first and simple, but in truth multiple, reason* for this is that our hosts at Cerisy are artists in hospitality, but it is also that the theme of this conference is fundamentally the very secret of the duty of hospitality or of hospitality as the essence of culture, and finally it is also that the first duty of the host (in the double sense that the French *hôte* has of *guest* and *host* [in English in the original]) is to pay attention [*payer quelque attention*], as some here would say, and to pay homage or tribute to linguistic difference—I therefore thought I had to begin with an untranslatable sentence, getting myself all tied up already in Greek and in Latin. Others would say I had to begin with one of those passwords that one should not overuse. One would gain time—for life will have been so short—if one stopped speaking enigmatically or in shibboleths. Unless, of course, the password also allows one to gain time.

We can *receive* this already untranslatable sentence, *il y va d'un certain pas*, in more than one way. From the very first moment, the body of its statement, *pollakōs legomenon*, becomes plural. At least, it trembles in an unstable multiplicity as long as there is no context to stop us. In our starting point, however, we will dogmatically begin with the axiom according to which no context is absolutely saturable or saturating. No context can determine meaning to the point of exhaustiveness. Therefore the context neither produces nor guarantees impassable borders, thresholds that no step could pass [*trespasser*], *trespass* [in English in the original], as our anglophone friends would say. By recalling that this sentence, *il y va d'un certain pas*, is untranslatable, I am thinking not only of translatability into another language or into the other's language. For any translation into a non-French language would lose something of its potential multiplicity. And if one measures untranslatability, or rather the essential incompleteness of translating, against this remainder, well, then a similar border *already* passes between the several versions or interpretations of the same sentence in French. The shibboleth effect operates *within*, if one may still say so, the French language.

For example, and to limit myself to just two possibilities, *first of all* one can understand it, that is, one can paraphrase it in this way: he is going there at a certain pace [*il y va d'un certain pas*], that is to say, someone, the other, you or me, a man or a walking animal, in the masculine or the neuter, goes somewhere with a certain gait. Indeed, one will say: look, he is headed there at a certain pace [*il y va d'un certain pas*], he is going there (to town, to work, to combat, to bed—that is to say, to dream, to love, to die) with a certain gait [*pas*]. Here the third person pronoun "he" [*il*] has the grammatical value of a masculine personal subject.

But, *secondly*, one can also understand and paraphrase the same sentence, *il y va d'un certain pas*, in another way: what is concerned—neuter and impersonal subject—what one is talking about here, is the question of the step, the gait, the pace, the rhythm, the passage, or the traversal (which, moreover, happens to be the theme of the conference).

*Thirdly* and finally, this time in inaudible quotation marks or italics, one can also mention a mark of negation, by citing it: a certain "not" [*pas*] (*no, not, nicht, kein*).

This border of translation does not pass among various languages. It separates translation from itself, it separates translatability within one and the same language. A certain pragmatics thus inscribes this border *in the very inside of the so-called French language*. Like any pragmatics, it takes into consideration gestural operations and contextual marks that are not all and thoroughly discursive. Such is the shibboleth effect: it always exceeds meaning and the pure discursivity of meaning.

Babelization does not therefore wait for the multiplicity of languages. The identity of a language can only affirm itself as identity to itself by opening itself to the hospitality of a difference from itself or of a difference with itself. Condition of the self, such a difference *from* and *with* itself would then be its very thing, the *pragma* of its pragmatics: the stranger at home, the invited or the one who is called. The *at home* [*chez-soi*] as the host's gift recalls a being at home [*chez-soi*] (*being at home, homely, heimisch, heimlich*) that is given by a hospitality more ancient than the inhabitant himself. As though the inhabitant himself were always staying in the inhabitant's home, the one who invites and receives truly begins by receiving hospitality from the guest to whom he thinks he is giving hospitality. It is as if in truth he were received by the one he thinks he is receiving. Wouldn't the consequences of this be infinite? What does receiving amount to? Such an infinity would then be lost in the abyss of receiving, of reception, or of the receptacle, the abyss of that *endekhomenon* whose enigma cuts into the entire meditation of *Timaeus* concerning the address of the *Khōra* (*eis khōran*). *Endekhomai* means to take upon oneself, in oneself, at home, with oneself, to receive, welcome, accept, and admit something other than oneself, the other than oneself. One can take it as a certain experience of hospitality, as the crossing of the threshold by the guest who must be at once called, desired, and expected, but also always free to come or not to come. It is indeed a question of admitting, accepting, and inviting. But let us not forget that in the passive or impersonal sense (*endekhetai*), the same verb names that which is acceptable, admissible, permitted, and, more generally, possible, the contrary of the "it is not permitted," "it is not necessary to," "it is necessary not to," or "it is not possible" (e.g., to cross the "limits of truth"). *Endekhomenōs* means: insofar as it is possible. Indeed, concerning the threshold of death, we are engaged here toward a certain possibility of the impossible.

The crossing of borders always announces itself according to the movement of a certain step [*pas*]—and of the step that crosses a line. An indivisible line. And one always assumes the institution of such an indivisibility. Customs, police, visa or passport, passenger identification—all of that is established upon this institution of the indivisible, the institution therefore of the step that is related to it, whether the step crosses it or not. Consequently, where the figure of the step is refused to intuition, where the identity or indivisibility of a line (*finis* or *peras*) is compromised, the identity to oneself and therefore the possible identification of an intangible edge—the crossing of the line—becomes a *problem*. There is a *problem* as soon as the edge-line is threatened. And it is threatened from its first tracing. This tracing can only institute the line by dividing it intrinsically into two sides. There is a *problem* as soon as this intrinsic division divides the relation to itself of the border and therefore divides the being-one-self of anything.

PROBLEM: I choose the word *problem* deliberately for *two reasons.*

1. First, to sacrifice a little bit more to Greek and to the experience of translation: in sum, *problēma* can signify *projection* or *protection*, that which one poses or throws in front of oneself, either as the projection of a project, of a task to accomplish, or as the protection created by a substitute, a prosthesis that we put forth in order to represent, replace, shelter, or dissimulate ourselves, or so as to hide something unavowable—like a shield (*problēma* also means

shield, clothing as barrier or guard-barrier) behind which one guards oneself *in secret* or *in shelter* in case of danger. Every border is *problematic* in these two senses.

2. I keep the word *problem* for another reason: so as to put this word in tension with another Greek word, *aporia*, which I chose a long time ago as a title for this occasion, without really knowing where I was going, except that I knew what was going to be at stake in this word was the "not knowing where to go." It had to be a matter of [*il devait y aller du*] the nonpassage, or rather from the experience of the nonpassage, the experience of what happens [*se passe*] and is fascinating [*passionne*] in this nonpassage, paralyzing us in this separation in a way that is not necessarily negative: before a door, a threshold, a border, a line, or simply the edge or the approach of the other as such. It should be a matter of [*devrait y aller du*] what, in sum, appears to block our way or to separate us in the very place where *it would no longer be possible to constitute a problem*, a project, or a projection, that is, at the point where the very project or the problematic task becomes impossible and where we are exposed, absolutely without protection, without problem, and without prosthesis, without possible substitution, singularly exposed in our absolute and absolutely naked uniqueness, that is to say, disarmed, delivered to the other, incapable even of sheltering ourselves behind what could still protect the interiority of a secret. There, in sum, in this place of aporia, *there is no longer any problem*. Not that, alas or fortunately, the solutions have been given, but because one could no longer even find a problem that would constitute itself and that one would keep in front of oneself, as a presentable object or project, as a protective representative or a prosthetic substitute, as some kind of border still to cross or behind which to protect oneself.

I gave in to the word *aporias,* in the plural, without really knowing where I was going and if something would come to pass, allowing me to pass with it, except that I recalled that, for many years now, the old, worn-out Greek term *aporia,* this tired word of philosophy and of logic, has often imposed itself upon me, and recently it has done so even more often. Thus, I speak here in memory of this word, as of someone with whom I would have lived a long time, even though in this case one cannot speak of a decision or a contract. It happened in a number of different contexts, but with a formalizable regularity about which I would like to say a few words before attempting to go—further, closer, or elsewhere. I would certainly not want to impose upon you a laborious or self-indulgent return to certain trajectories or impasses of the past. Rather, I would like to situate, from very far away and very high up, in the most abstract way, in a few sentences, and in the form of an index or a long note at the bottom of the page, the places of aporia in which I have found myself, let us say, regularly tied up, indeed, paralyzed. I was then trying to move not against or out of the impasse but, in another way, *according to* another thinking of the aporia, one perhaps more enduring. It is the obscure way of this "according to the aporia" that I will try to determine today. And I hope that the index I just mentioned will help situate my discourse better.

The word "aporia" appears in person in Aristotle's famous text, *Physics IV* (217b), which reconstitutes the aporia of time *dia tōn exoterikōn logōn*. Allow me to recall the short text that, twenty-five years ago, I devoted to a note on time in *Being and Time* ("*Ousia* and *Grammē*: Note on a Note from *Being and Time*," in *Margins of Philosophy*): already dealing with Heidegger, as I shall also do today, but in a different way, this short text treated the question of the present, of presence and of the presentation of the present, of time, of being, and above all of nonbeing, more precisely of a certain *impossibility* as nonviability, as nontrack or barred path. It concerns the impossible or the impracticable. (*Diaporeō* is Aristotle's term here; it means "I'm stuck [*dans l'embarras*], I cannot get out, I'm helpless.") Therefore, for example—and it is more than just one example among others—it is impossible to determine time both as entity and as nonentity. And with the motif of the nonentity, or of nothingness, the motif of death is never very far away. (Even though Levinas, in a fundamental debate, reproaches Heidegger, as well as an entire tradition, for wrongly thinking death, in its very

essence and in the first place, as annihilation.) The now is and is
not what it is. More precisely, it only "scarcely" (*amudrōs*) is what it
is. Insofar as it has been, it no longer is. But insofar as it will be, as
future to come or as death—which will be my themes today—it is
not yet. By insisting upon the fact that "the aporetic is an exoteric"[6]
and that Aristotle, "while acknowledging that this argument clar-
ifies nothing (218a)" "repeats its aporia without deconstructing it"
(p. 50), I was then trying to demonstrate, thereby going in the
direction of Heidegger, that the philosophical tradition, in particular from Kant to Hegel, only inherited this aporetic: "the Aristo-
telian aporia is understood, thought, and assimilated into that
which is properly *dialectical.* It suffices—and it is necessary—to take
things in the other sense and from the other side in order to
conclude that the Hegelian dialectic is but the repetition, the
paraphrastic reedition of an exoteric aporia, the brilliant formulation of a vulgar paradox" (p. 43). But instead of stopping with a
mere confirmation of the Heideggerian diagnosis, which indeed
sees in the whole tradition, from Aristotle to Hegel, a hegemony of
the vulgar concept of time insofar as it privileges the now (*nun,*
*Jetzt*), I oriented this very confirmation toward another suggestion,
even while supporting it. Allow me to recall it because I may make
a similar, albeit different, gesture today on the subject of death
according to Heidegger. The simple question from which I was
trying to draw the consequences (and from which one may never
finish drawing them) would be this: What if there was no other
concept of time than the one that Heidegger calls "vulgar"? What
if, consequently, opposing another concept to the "vulgar" concept
were itself impracticable, nonviable, and impossible? What if it was
the same for death, for a vulgar concept of death? What if the
exoteric aporia therefore remained in a certain way irreducible,
calling for an endurance, or shall we rather say an *experience* other
than that consisting in opposing, from both sides of an indivisible
line, an other concept, a nonvulgar concept, to the so-called vulgar
concept?

What would such an *experience* be? The word also means passage, traversal, endurance, and rite of passage, but can be a traversal

without line and without indivisible border. Can it ever concern, precisely (in all the domains where the questions of decision and of responsibility that concern the border—ethics, law, politics, etc.—are posed), surpassing an aporia, crossing an oppositional line *or else* apprehending, enduring, and putting, in a different way, the experience of the aporia to a test? And is it an issue here of an *either/or*? Can one speak—and if so, in what sense—of an *experience of the aporia*? An experience *of the aporia as such*? Or vice versa: Is an experience possible that would not be an experience of the aporia?

If it was necessary to recall at some length this analysis of the Aristotelian-Hegelian aporetic of time, carried out with Heidegger, it is because the theme of our conference was already noted there insistently: the border as limit (*oros, Grenze*: these determinations of the present now, of the *nun* or of the *Jetzt* that Heidegger underlines) or the border as tracing (*grammē, Linie*, etc.). However, I will not elaborate the numerous instances where this theme has recurred since then: the aporetology or aporetography in which I have not ceased to struggle ever since; the paradoxical limitrophy of "Tympan" and of the margins [*marges*], the levels [*marches*], or the marks [*marques*] of undecidability—and the interminable list of all the so-called undecidable quasi-concepts that are so many aporetic places or dislocations; the *double bind* [in English in the original] and all the double bands and columns in *Glas*, the work of impossible mourning, the impracticable opposition between incorporation and introjection in "Fors," in *Mémoires for Paul de Man* (particularly pp. 132 and 147), and in *Psyché: Inventions de l'autre* (where deconstruction is explicitly defined as a certain aporetic experience of the impossible, p. 27); the step [*pas*] and paralysis in *Parages*, the "nondialectizable contradiction" (p. 72), the birth date that "only happens by effacing itself" in *Schibboleth* (p. 89 and following), iterability, that is, the conditions of possibility as conditions of impossibility, which recurs almost everywhere, in particular in "Signature Event Context" (*Margins*) and in *Limited Inc.*, the invention of the other as the impossible in *Psyché*, the seven antinomies of the philosophical discipline in *Du droit à la philosophie* (pp.

55, 515, 521), the gift as the impossible (*Donner le temps*, p. 19 and following); and above all, in the places where questions of juridical, ethical, or political responsibility also concern geographical, national, ethnic, or linguistic borders, I would have been tempted to insist upon the most recent formalization of this aporetic in *The Other Heading* (written at the time of the Gulf War). There, at a precise moment, without giving in to any dialectic, I used the term "aporia" (p. 116) for a *single duty* that recurrently duplicates itself interminably, fissures itself, and contradicts itself without remaining the same, that is, concerning the only and single "double, contradictory imperative" (p. 77). I suggested that a sort of nonpassive endurance of the aporia was the condition of responsibility and of decision. Aporia, rather than antinomy: the word *antinomy* imposed itself up to a certain point since, in terms of the law (*nomos*), contradictions or antagonisms among equally imperative laws were at stake. However, the antinomy here better deserves the name of aporia insofar as it is neither an "apparent or illusory" antinomy, nor a dialectizable contradiction in the Hegelian or Marxist sense, nor even a "transcendental illusion in a dialectic of the Kantian type," but instead an interminable experience. Such an experience must remain such if one wants to think, to make come or to let come any event of decision or of responsibility. The most general and therefore most indeterminate form of this double and single duty is that a responsible decision must obey an "it is necessary" that owes nothing, it must obey a *duty that owes nothing, that must owe nothing in order to be a duty*, a duty that has no debt to pay back, a duty without debt and therefore without duty.[7]

In more recent texts ("Passions" and "Donner la mort"), I have pursued the necessarily aporetic analysis of a duty as *over-duty* whose *hubris* and essential excess dictate transgressing not only the action that *conforms to duty* (*Pflichtmässig*) but also the action undertaken *out of the sense of duty* (*aus Pflicht*), that is, what Kant defines as the very condition of morality. Duty must be such an over-duty, which demands acting without duty, without rule or norm (therefore without law) under the risk of seeing the so-called responsible decision become again the merely technical application of a concept and therefore of a presentable knowledge. In order to be responsible and truly decisive, a decision should not limit itself to putting into operation a determinable or determining knowledge, the consequence of some preestablished order. But, conversely, who would call a decision that is without rule, without norm, without determinable or determined law, a decision? Who will answer for it as if for a responsible decision, and before whom? Who will dare call duty a duty that owes nothing, or, better (or, worse), that *must owe nothing*? It is necessary, therefore, that the decision and responsibility for it be taken, interrupting the relation to any *presentable* determination but still maintaining a presentable relation to the interruption and to what it interrupts. Is that possible? Is it possible once the interruption always resembles the mark of a borderly edge, the mark of a threshold not to be trespassed?

This formulation of the paradox and of the impossible therefore calls upon a figure that resembles a structure of temporality, an instantaneous dissociation from the present, a *différance* in being-with-itself of the present, of which I gave then some examples. These examples were not fortuitously political. It was not by accident that they concerned the question of Europe, of European borders and of the border of the political, of *politeia* and of the State as European concepts. Nine or eleven times, they involved the same aporetic duty; they involved ten—plus or minus one—commandments considered as examples in an infinite series in which the ten could only count a series of examples. In the end, the entire analysis concerned the very logic of exemplarism in any national or nationalist affirmation, particularly in Europe's relation to itself. In order to gain time, and before closing this backtracking that has the form of premises—forgive me, I needed to do so—I will rapidly mention the first seven aporias that concern the theme of this conference. Each of them puts to test a *passage*, both an impossible and a necessary passage, and two apparently heterogeneous borders. The first type of border passes among *contents* (things, objects, referents: territories, countries, states, nations, cultures, languages, etc.), or between Europe and some non-Europe, for example. The other type of borderly limit would pass between a *concept* (singularly that of duty) and an other, according to the bar of an oppositional logic. Each time the decision concerns the choice between the relation to an other who is *its* other (that is to say, an other that can be opposed in a couple) and the relation to a wholly, non-opposable, other, that is, an other that is no longer *its* other. What is at stake in the first place is therefore not the crossing of a given border. Rather, at stake is the *double concept of the border*, from which this aporia comes to be determined:

> The *duty* to respond to the call of European memory, to recall what has been promised under the name Europe, to re-identify Europe—this *duty* is without common measure with all that is generally understood by the name duty, though it could be shown that all other duties presuppose it in silence. [To put it otherwise, Europe would not only be the object or theme of a duty-to-remember and duty-to-keep-a-promise; Europe would be the singular place of the formation of the concept of duty and the origin, the possibility itself of an infinite promise.]
>
> This *duty* also dictates opening Europe, from the heading that is divided because it is also a shoreline: opening it into that which is not, never was, and never will be Europe.
>
> The *same duty* also dictates welcoming foreigners in order not only to integrate them but to recognize and accept their alterity: two concepts of hospitality that today divide our European and national consciousness.
>
> The *same duty* dictates *criticizing* ("in-both-theory-and-in-practice," and relentlessly) a totalitarian dogmatism that, under the pretense of putting an end to capital, destroyed democracy and the European heritage. But it also dictates criticizing a religion of capital that institutes its dogmatism under new guises, which we must also learn to identify—for this is the future itself, and there will be none otherwise.
>
> The *same duty* dictates cultivating the virtue of such *critique, of the critical idea, the critical tradition*, but also submitting it, beyond critique and questioning, to a deconstructive genealogy that thinks and exceeds it without yet compromising it.
>
> The *same duty* dictates assuming the European, and *uniquely* Euro-

pean, heritage of an idea of democracy, while also recognizing that this idea, like that of international law, is never simply given, that its status is not even that of a regulative idea in the Kantian sense, but rather something that remains to be thought and *to come* [*à venir*]: not something that is certain to happen tomorrow, not the democracy (national or international, state or trans-state) of the *future*, but a democracy that must have the structure of a promise—*and thus the memory of that which carries the future, the to come, here and now.*

The *same duty* dictates respecting differences, idioms, minorities, singularities, but also the universality of formal law, the desire for translation, agreement, and univocity, the law of the majority, opposition to racism, nationalism, and xenophobia.[8]

Why this language, which does not fortuitously resemble that of negative theology? How to justify the choice of *negative form* (*aporia*) to designate a duty that, through the impossible or the impracticable, nonetheless announces itself in an affirmative fashion? Because one must avoid good conscience at all costs. Not only good conscience as the grimace of an indulgent vulgarity, but quite simply the assured form of self-consciousness: good conscience as subjective certainty is incompatible with the absolute risk that every promise, every engagement, and every responsible decision— if there are such—must run. To protect the decision or the responsibility by knowledge, by some theoretical assurance, or by the certainty of being right, of being on the side of science, of consciousness or of reason, is to transform this experience into the deployment of a program, into a technical application of a rule or a norm, or into the subsumption of a determined "case." All these are conditions that must never be abandoned, of course, but that, as such, are only the guardrail of a responsibility to whose calling they remain radically heterogeneous. The affirmation that announced itself through a negative form was therefore the necessity of *experience* itself, the experience of the aporia (and these two words that tell of the passage and the nonpassage are thereby coupled in an aporetic fashion) as endurance or as passion, as interminable resistance or remainder. I'll give a final quote regarding this formal negativity:

One could multiply the examples of this double duty. It would be necessary above all to discern the unprecedented forms that it is taking today in Europe. And not only to accept but to claim this putting to the test of the antinomy (in the forms, for example, of the double constraint, the undecidable, the performative contradiction, etc.). It would be necessary to recognize both the typical or recurring form and the inexhaustible singularization—without which there will never be any event, decision, responsibility, ethics, or politics. These conditions can only take a negative *form* (without X there would not be Y). One can be certain only of this negative form. As soon as it is converted into positive certainty ("on this condition, there will surely have been event, decision, responsibility, ethics, or politics"), one can be sure that one is beginning to be deceived, indeed beginning to deceive the other.

We are speaking here with names (event, decision, responsibility, ethics, politics—Europe) of "things" that can only exceed (and *must* exceed) the order of theoretical determination, of knowledge, certainty, judgment, and of statements in the form of "this is that," in other words, more generally and essentially, the order of the *present* or of *presentation*. Each time they are reduced to what they must exceed, error, recklessness, the unthought, and irresponsibility are given the so very presentable face of good conscience. (And it is also necessary to say that the serious, unsmiling mask of a declared bad conscience often exhibits only a supplementary ruse; for good conscience has, by definition, inexhaustible resources.)[9]

A plural logic of the aporia thus takes shape. It appears to be paradoxical enough so that the partitioning [*partage*] among multiple figures of aporia does not oppose figures to each other, but instead installs the haunting of the one in the other. In one case, the nonpassage resembles an impermeability; it would stem from the opaque existence of an uncrossable border: a door that does not open or that only opens according to an unlocatable condition, according to the inaccessible secret of some shibboleth. Such is the case for all closed borders (exemplarily during war). In another case, the nonpassage, the impasse or aporia, stems from the fact that there is no limit. There is not yet or there is no longer a border to cross, no opposition between two sides: the limit is too porous, permeable, and indeterminate. There is no longer a home [*chez-soi*] and a not-home [*chez l'autre*], whether in peacetime (exemplarily according to the rule of universal peace, even beyond the Kantian sense that presupposes a public, interstate system of rights[10]) or in wartime—war and peace both appreciate, but appreciate *very little*, the borders. By definition, one always makes *very little* [*peu de cas*] of a border. And this "very little" would have to be formalized. Finally, the third type of aporia, the impossible, the antinomy, or the contradiction, is a nonpassage because its elementary milieu does not allow for something that could be called passage, step, walk, gait, displacement, or replacement, a kinesis in general. There is no more path (*odos, methodos, Weg,* or *Holzweg*). The impasse itself would be impossible. The coming or the future advent of the event would have no relation to the passage of what happens or comes to pass. In this case, there would be an aporia because there is not even any space for an aporia determined as experience of the step or of the edge, crossing or not of some line, relation to some spatial figure of the limit. No more movement or trajectory, no more *trans-* (transport, transposition, transgression, translation, and even transcendence). There would not even be any space for the aporia because of a lack of topographical conditions or, more radically, because of a lack of the topological condition itself. A subquestion to this limitless question would concern what affects these topographical or topological conditions when the speed of the panopticization of the earth—seen, inspected, surveyed, and transported by satellite images—even affects time, nearly annuls it, and indeed affects the space of passage between certain borders (this is one example among others of various so-called technical mutations that raise the same type of question).

In another conference it would have been necessary to explore these experiences of the edge or of the borderline under the names of what one calls the body proper and sexual difference. Today, in choosing the theme of death, of the syntagm "my death" and of the "limits of truth," to explore this subject, I will perhaps not speak of anything else under different names, but names matter.

Is my death possible?
Can we understand this question? Can I, myself, pose it? Am I allowed to talk about my death? What does the syntagm "my

death" mean? And why this expression "the syntagm 'my death' "?
You will agree that it is better, in this case, to name words or names,
that is, to stick with quotation marks. On the one hand, that
neutralizes an improper pathos. "My death" in quotation marks is
not necessarily mine; it is an expression that anybody can appropriate; it can circulate from one example to another. Regarding what
Seneca said about the brevity of life, Diderot tells us: "it is the story
of my life," it is my story. But it is not only his. Of course, if I say it
is not mine, then I seem to be assuming that I could know when to
say "my death" while speaking of mine. But this is more than
*problematic*, in the sense of this word that we analyzed above. If
death (we will return to this point later) names the very irre-
placeability of absolute singularity (no one can die in my place or in
the place of the other), then all the *examples* in the world can
precisely illustrate this singularity. Everyone's death, the death of all
those who can say "my death," is irreplaceable. So is "my life."
Every other is completely other. [*Tout autre est tout autre.*] Whence
comes a first exemplary complication of exemplarity: nothing is
more substitutable and yet nothing is less so than the syntagm "my
death." It is always a matter of a hapax, of a hapax legomenon, but
of what is only said *one time each time, indefinitely* only one time.
This is also true for everything that entails a first-person grammatical form. On the other hand, the quotation marks not only affect
this strange possessive (the uniqueness of the *hapax* "my"), but they
also signal the indeterminacy of the word "death." Fundamentally,
one knows perhaps neither the meaning nor the referent of this
word. It is well known that if there is one word that remains
absolutely unassignable or unassigning with respect to its concept
and to its thingness, it is the word "death." Less than for any other
noun, save "God"—and for good reason, since their association
here is probably not fortuitous—is it possible to attribute to the
noun "death," and above all to the expression "my death," a
concept or a reality that would constitute the object of an indis-
putably determining experience.

In order not to lose myself any longer in these preambulatory
detours, I will say very quickly now why "my death" will be the

subject of this small aporetic oration. First, I'll address the aporia, that is, the impossible, the impossibility, as what cannot pass [*passer*] or come to pass [*se passer*]: it is not even the *non-pas*, the not-step, but rather the deprivation of the *pas* (the privative form would be a kind of *a-pas*). I'll explain myself with some help from Heidegger's famous definition of death in *Being and Time*: "the possibility of the pure and simple impossibility for *Dasein*" (*Der Tod ist die Möglichkeit der schlechthinnigen Daseinsunmöglichkeit*) (§50, p. 250).[11] Second, I want to carry out such an explanation together with what is our common concern here, at Cerisy-la-Salle, during the time of this conference, namely, "the crossing [*passage*] of borders."

Up to this point, we have rightly privileged at least *three* types of *border limits*: *first,* those that separate territories, countries, nations, States, languages, and cultures (and the politico-anthropological disciplines that correspond to them); *second,* the separations and sharings [*partages*] between domains of discourse, for example, philosophy, anthropological sciences, and even theology, domains that have been represented, in an encyclopedia or in an ideal university, sometimes as ontological or onto-theological regions or territories, sometimes as knowledges or as disciplines of research; *third,* to these two kinds of border limits we have just added the lines of separation, demarcation, or opposition between conceptual determinations, the forms of the border that separates what are called concepts or *terms*—these are lines that necessarily intersect and overdetermine the first two kinds of terminality. Later I will suggest some terms in order to formalize somewhat these three kinds of limit—to be crossed or not to be transgressed.

Now where do we situate the syntagm "my death" as possibility and/or impossibility of passage? (As we shall see, the mobile slash between and/or, and/and, or/and, or/or, is a singular border, simultaneously conjunctive, disjunctive, and undecidable.) "My death," this syntagm that relates the possible to the impossible, can be figured flashing like a sort of indicator-light (a light at a border) installed at a customs booth, between all the borders that I have just named: between cultures, countries, languages, but also between the areas of knowledge or the disciplines, and, finally, between conceptual de-terminations. A light flashes at every border, where it is awake and watches [*ça veille*]. One can always see there a nightwatchman [*du veilleur*] or a nightlight [*de la veilleuse*].

Let us start with a fact that is overwhelming, well-known, and immensely documented: there are cultures of death. In crossing a border, one changes death [*on change la mort*]. One exchanges death [*on change de mort*]; one no longer speaks the same death where one no longer speaks the same language. The relation to death is not the same on this side of the Pyrenees as it is on the other side. Often, moreover, in crossing a culture's border, one passes from a figure of death as trespass—passage of a line, transgression of a border, or step beyond [*pas au-delà*] life—to another figure of the border between life and death. Every culture is characterized by its way of apprehending, dealing with, and, one could say, "living" death as trespass. Every culture has its own funerary rites, its representations of the dying, its ways of mourning or burying, and its own evaluation of the price of existence, of collective as well as individual life. Furthermore, this culture of death can be transformed even within what we believe we can identify as a single culture, sometimes as a single nation, a single language, or a single religion (but I explained above how the principle of such an identification appears to be threatened in its very principle or to be exposed to ruin right from the outset, that is, to be exposed to death). One can speak of a history of death, and, as you know, it has been done, for the West at least. The fact that, to my knowledge, it has only been done in the West (even though a Westerner, Maurice Pinguet, devoted to this question a study that was both genealogical and sociological, in *La Mort volontaire au Japon* [Paris: Gallimard, 1984]), that is to say, the fact that it has only been done "here at home," here where we are, does not mean that there is no history of death elsewhere or that no one has written any—unless the idea of a history and of a history of death is itself a Western idea in a sense that will be clarified later. For the record, I will only cite one or two titles from the immense library of work devoted to the history of death. They are French works, which is the first restriction, and they are recent, which is another unjustifiably arbitrary choice. First, the *Essais sur l'histoire de la mort en Occident du Moyen Age à nos jours* and *L'Homme devant la mort,* by Philippe Ariès. Like his *Western Attitudes Towards Death* (Johns Hopkins University Press, 1974), these studies, which date from 1975 and 1977 respectively, clearly show the limits within which such a history is framed. The author, who calls himself a "historian of death" (*L'Homme devant la mort,* p. 9), focuses on what is, in sum, a very short and dense sequence in the time span of the Christian West. With all due respect for the richness, the necessity, and at times the beauty of works such as these, which are also masterpieces of their genre, I must nevertheless recall the strict limits of these anthropological histories. This word ("limit") not only designates the external limits that the historian gives himself for methodological purposes (death in the West from the Middle Ages to the present, for example), but also certain nonthematized closures, edges [*bordures*] whose concept is never formulated in these works. First, there is the semantic or onto-phenomenological type of limit: the historian knows, thinks he knows, or grants to himself the unquestioned knowledge of what death is, of what being-dead means; consequently, he grants to himself all the criteriology that will allow him to identify, recognize, select, or delimit the objects of his inquiry or the thematic field of his anthropologico-historical knowledge. The question of the meaning of death and of the word "death," the question "What is death in general?" or "What is the experience of death?" and the question of knowing *if* death "is"—and *what* death "is"—all remain radically absent *as questions.* From the outset these questions are assumed to be answered by this anthropologico-historical knowledge as such, at the moment when it institutes itself and gives itself its limits. This assumption takes the form of an "it is self-explanatory": everybody knows what one is talking about when one names death.

In these texts foaming with knowledge, one never finds any precaution like the one Heidegger takes, for example, when, intending to recall that it is impossible to *die for the other* in the sense of "to die in his place," even if one dies for the other by offering his own death to the other, he leaves the small word "is" in quotation marks in the following sentence: "By its very essence, death is in every case mine, insofar as it 'is' at all" ("Der Tod ist, sofern es 'ist,' wesensmäßig je der meine") (*Being and Time*, p. 240). Citing Heidegger here or there is not sufficient to put such treasures of anthropological or cultural knowledge to the test of these semantic, phenomenological, or ontological questions, and it is especially not enough to cite Heidegger as an illustration or as an authoritative argument (which often amounts to the same thing). This is what Louis-Vincent Thomas does, in the second book that I want to mention, his rich *Anthropologie de la mort* (Payot, 1975). One could multiply the examples, but there is no time for that. At the beginning of a chapter entitled "The Experience of Death: Reality, Limit" (p. 223), Thomas writes: "'No sooner is the human being born,' writes M. Heidegger, 'than he is already old enough to die.' Does this incontestable (metaphysical) truth, verified by all the givens of biological sciences and attested to by demography, mean anything at the level of lived experience?" The sentence that Thomas quotes is incorrectly attributed to Heidegger. It recalls Seneca's remark about the permanent imminence of death, right from birth, and the essential immaturity of the human who is dying. In the opening of his existential analysis of death, Heidegger also distinguishes the death of *Dasein* from its end (*Ende*) and above all from its maturation or ripeness (*Reife*). *Dasein* does not need to mature when death occurs. That is why life will always have been so short. Whether one understands it as achievement or as accomplishment, the final maturity of a fruit or of a biological organism is a limit, an end (*Ende*; one could also say a *telos* or *terma*), hence a border, which *Dasein* is always in a position of surpassing. *Dasein* is the very transgression of this borderline. It may well have passed its maturity before the end (*vor dem Ende schon überschritten haben kann*), Heidegger says. For the most part, *Dasein* ends in unfulfillment, or else by having disintegrated and been used up ("Zumeist endet es in der Unvollendung oder aber zerfallen und verbraucht"; *Being and Time*, p. 244). Thomas should have avoided attributing to Heidegger a line that the latter quotes

(p. 245), taking it from *Der Ackermann aus Böhmen* ("sobald ein Mensch zum Leben kommt, sogleich ist er alt genug zu sterben"). Heidegger uses this quote at the very moment when he distinguishes the death of *Dasein* from any other end, from any other limit. This crucial distinction, which Heidegger considers indispensable, allows him to situate his existential analysis of death *before* any "metaphysics of death" and *before* all biology. Thomas, however, thinks that he is citing Heidegger and that he can speak of an "incontestable (metaphysical) truth" that has been verified "by all the givens of biological sciences" as well as by "demography."

Yet Heidegger recalls that the existential analysis of death can and must precede, on the one hand, any metaphysics of death and, on the other, all biology, psychology, theodicy, or theology of death (p. 248). Saying exactly the opposite of what Thomas makes him say, Heidegger puts into operation a logic of *presupposition.* All the disciplines thus named, and thereby identified within their regional borders, notably "metaphysics" and "biology," not to mention "demography," necessarily presuppose a meaning of death, a preunderstanding of what death is or of what the word "death" means. The theme of the existential analysis is to explain and make explicit this ontological preunderstanding. If one wants to translate this situation in terms of disciplinary or regional borders, of domains of knowledge, then one will say that the delimitation of the fields of anthropological, historical, biological, demographic, and even theological knowledge presupposes a nonregional ontophenomenology that not only does not let itself be enclosed within the borders of these domains, but furthermore does not let itself be enclosed within cultural, linguistic, national, or religious borders either, and not even within sexual borders, which crisscross all the others.

To put it quickly—in passing, and in an anticipatory way—the logic of this Heideggerian gesture interests me here. It does so in its exemplarity. However, I only want to assert the force of its necessity and go with it as far as possible, apparently against anthropological confusions and presumptions, so as to try to bring to light several aporias that are internal to the Heideggerian discourse. At stake for

me would be approaching the place where such aporias risk paralyzing the ontological, hierarchical, and territorial apparatus to
which Heidegger lends credit. These aporias risk interrupting the
very possibility of its functioning and leading it to ruin. Death
would be the name, one of the names, of this threat, which no
doubt takes over from what Heidegger himself very early on called
"ruination."

But we are not there yet; this will come only near the end. For
the moment, let us remain close to this border dispute. It arises here
between, on the one hand, a comparative anthropo-thanatology
("anthropothanatology" is the title proposed by Thomas, who
insists on its essentially "comparative" aim, pp. 530–531) and, on
the other hand, an existential analysis.

When Heidegger suggests a delimitation of the borders (*Abgrenzung*) of existential analysis (*Being and Time*, §49), he relies on a
classical argument within the philosophical tradition. In turn dialectical, transcendental, and ontological, it is always the argument
of presupposition (*Voraussetzung*). Whether it concerns plants,
animals, or humans, the ontico-biological knowledge about the
span of life and about the mechanisms of death *presupposes* an
ontological problematic. This ontological problematic underlies
(*zugrundeliegt*) all biological research. What always remains to be
asked (*zu fragen bleibt*), says Heidegger, is how the essence of death
is defined in terms of that of life. Insofar as they are ontical
research, biology and anthropology have already and always decided (*immer schon entschieden*). They have decided without even
asking the question, hence by precipitating the answer and by
presupposing an ontological elucidation that had not taken place.
This precipitation does not simply stem from a speculative failure or from the betrayal of a principle of philosophical legitimacy [*droit*] concerning what must come first, whether *de jure* or
methodologically. It also leads to apparently empirical or techno-
juridical confusions about what the state of death is, confusions
that are increasingly serious today. These questions of legitimacy
[*questions de droit*] are no longer only questions concerning the
philosophical order of *de jure* and *de facto*. They impinge upon

legal medicine, the politics of gerontology, the norms concerning the surgical prolongation of life and euthanasia, and upon several other questions that will be addressed later.

Heidegger multiplies the programmatical propositions concerning the *order*—that is, the subordination of questions—of what is prior and *superordinate* (*vorgeordnet*) or, on the contrary, ulterior and subordinate (*nachgeordnet*). Such propositions appear to be firm. Ontical knowledge (anthropological or biological) naively puts into operation more or less clear conceptual presuppositions (*Vorbegriffe*) about life and death. It therefore requires a preparatory sketch, a new *Vorzeichnung* in terms of an ontology of *Dasein*, an ontology that is itself preliminary, "superordinate," prior to an ontology of life: "Within the ontology of Dasein, which is *superordinate* to an ontology of life [*Innerhalb der einer Ontologie des Lebens* vorgeordneten *Ontologie des Daseins*; Heidegger emphasizes *superordinate*: the ontology of *Dasein* is legitimately and logically prior to an ontology of life], the existential analysis of death is, in turn, *subordinate* to a characterization of *Dasein's* basic state (*Grundverfassung*)" (p. 247). This characteristic, that is, the existential analysis of *Dasein*, is thus an *absolute priority*, and then an existential analysis of death, which is itself a part of this ontology of *Dasein*, comes to be subordinate to it. In turn, this ontology of *Dasein* is presupposed by an ontology of life that it thus legitimately precedes. If Heidegger uses the expressions *Dasein* and analysis of *Dasein*, it is because he does not yet allow himself any philosophical knowledge concerning what man is as *animal rationale*, or concerning the ego, consciousness, the soul, the subject, the person, and so forth, which are all presuppositions of metaphysics or of ontical knowledge, such as anthropo-thanatology or biology. A hierarchical order thus delimits the field; it rigorously superordinates or subordinates the questions, themes, and, in fact, the ontological regions. According to Heidegger, these regions are legitimately separated by pure, rigorous, and indivisible borders. An order is thus structured by *uncrossable* edges. Such edges can be crossed, and they are *in fact* crossed all the time, but they *should* not be. The hierarchy of this order is governed by the concern to think what the death proper to *Dasein* is, that is, *Dasein*'s "properly dying" (*eigentlich sterben*). This "properly dying" belongs to the proper and authentic being-able of *Dasein*, that is, to that to which one must testify and attest (*Bezeugung*, §54).

At stake for me here is approaching a certain enigmatic relation among dying, testifying, and surviving. We can already foresee it: if the attestation of this "properly dying" or if the property of this death proper to *Dasein* was compromised in its rigorous limits, then the entire apparatus of these edges would become problematic, and along with it the very project of an analysis of *Dasein*, as well as everything that, with its professed methodology, the analysis legitimately [*en droit*] conditions. All these conditions of legitimacy [*conditions de droit*] concern border crossings: what authorizes them here, what prohibits them there, what ordinates, subordinates, or superordinates the ones over the others.

Heidegger thus suggests an ontological delimitation among the fields of inquiry concerning death. This delimitation seems all the more abyssal because it concerns limits about questions of the limit, more precisely, questions of the ends, of the modes of ending (*enden, verenden*), and of the limit that separates the simple *ending* (*enden*) from *properly dying* (*eigentlich sterben*). But as we shall see, there is more than one limit. That is why we began, from our very first words, by speaking about the ends, *de finibus*. That was not a roundabout way of recalling the ends of man, as if after a long decade, the present conference was not able to rid itself of the same subject, of an indestructible [*increvable*] subject. If one takes it literally, the death of *Dasein* is not an end of man. Between the two there is a singular, improbable, and perhaps divisible limit that passes, and it is the limit of the *ending*, the place where, in a way, the ending ends. What comes to pass, what happens and what am I saying when I say *end* [*finis*], for example when I say, addressing someone or sending him a note, "*end it*," "*end this now*," or "*that's the end of you*"?

Heidegger says that he has called the end of the living, the ending of the living (*das Enden von Lebendem*), "perishing," *Verenden* (*Das Enden von Lebendem nannten wir Verenden*, p. 247). This *Verenden* is the ending, the way of ending or of coming to the end that all living things share. They all eventually kick the bucket [*ils crèvent*]. In everyday German, *verenden* also means to die, to succumb, to kick the bucket, but since that is clearly not what Heidegger means by properly dying (*eigentlich sterben*), by the dying proper to *Dasein*, *verenden* must therefore not be translated by "dying" in order to respect what Heidegger intends to convey. That is why the translators hesitate between translating *verenden* by "arrêt de vie" (Vezin, stoppage of life), by "périr" (Martineau, to perish), or by "perishing" in English (Macquarrie-Robinson).[12]

I prefer "perishing." Why? Just because it turns up twice instead of once among these translations? No, rather because the verb "to perish" retains something of *per*, of the passage of the limit, of the traversal marked in Latin by the *pereo, perire* (which means exactly: to leave, disappear, pass—on the other side of life, *transire*). *To perish* crosses the line and passes near the lines of our conference, even if it loses a little of this sense of ending and of corruption perhaps marked by the *ver* of *verenden*.

Before noting a further complication in the modalities of ending (*Enden*), one should consider that the distinction between *perishing* and *dying* has been established, as far as Heidegger is concerned, as he will never call it into question again, not even in order to complicate it.

As is self-evident, this distinction between, on the one hand, death (*der Tod*) or properly dying (*eigentlich sterben*) and, on the other hand, perishing (*verenden*) cannot be reduced to a terminological decision. It involves decisive conceptual questions for whoever wants to approach what it is, properly, to die or what properly dying is. Above all, and precisely for that reason, it involves the very condition of an existential analysis of *Dasein*, of a *Dasein* that, as we shall see, reaches its most proper possibility and becomes most properly what it is at the very point where it can claim to *testify* to it, in its anticipation of death. If, in its very principle, the rigor of this distinction were compromised, weakened, or parasited on both sides of what it is supposed to dissociate (*verenden/eigentlich sterben*), then (and you can guess that I am heading toward such a possibility) the entire project of the analysis of *Dasein*, in its essential conceptuality, would be, if not discredited, granted another status than the one generally attributed to it. I am thus increasingly inclined to read ultimately this great, inexhaustible book in the following way: as an event that, at least in the final analysis, would no longer simply stem from ontological necessity or demonstration. It would never submit to logic, phenomenology, or ontology, which it nonetheless invokes. Nor would it ever submit to a "rigorous science" (in the sense that Husserl intended it), not even to thought (*Denken*) as that which parallels the path of the poem (*Dichten*), and finally, not even to an incredible poem—which I would be nevertheless inclined to believe, without, however, stopping on this point for obvious reasons. The event of this interrupted book would be irreducible to these categories, indeed to the categories that Heidegger himself never stopped articulating. In order to welcome into thought and into history such a "work," the event has to be thought otherwise. *Being and Time* would belong neither to science, nor to philosophy, nor to poetics. Such is perhaps the case for every work worthy of its name: there, what puts thinking into operation exceeds its own borders or what thinking itself intends to present of these borders. The work exceeds itself, it surpasses the limits of the concept of itself that it claims to have properly while presenting itself. But if the event of this work thus exceeds its own borders, the borders that its discourse seems to give to itself (for example, "those of an existential analysis of *Dasein* in the transcendental horizon of time"), then it would do so precisely at this locus where it *experiences the aporia*— and perhaps its premature interruption, its very prematurity.

It is with regard to death that we shall approach this aporetic structure in *Being and Time*. But the question of knowing what it means "to experience the aporia," indeed to put into operation the aporia, remains. It is not necessarily a failure or a simple paralysis, the sterile negativity of the impasse. It is neither stopping at it nor overcoming it. (When someone suggests to you a solution for escaping an impasse, you can be almost sure that he is ceasing to understand, assuming that he had understood anything up to that point.)

Let us ask: *what takes place, what comes to pass* with the aporia? Is it possible to undergo or to experience the aporia, the aporia *as such*? Is it then a question of the aporia *as such*? Of a scandal arising to suspend a certain viability? Does one then pass through this aporia? Or is one immobilized before the threshold, to the point of having to turn around and seek out another way, the way without method or outlet of a *Holzweg* or a turning (*Kehre*) that could turn the aporia—all such possibilities of wandering? What takes place with the aporia? What we are apprehending here concerning what takes place also touches upon the event as that which arrives at the river's shore [*arrive à la rive*], approaches the shore [*aborde la rive*], or passes the edge [*passe le bord*]—another way of happening and coming to pass by surpassing [*outrepassant*]. All of these are possibilities of the "coming to pass" when it meets a limit. Perhaps nothing ever comes to pass except on the line of a transgression, the death [*trépas*] of some "trespassing" [in English in the original].

What is the event that most arrives [*l'événement le plus arrivant*]? What is the *arrivant* that makes the event arrive?[13] I was recently taken by this word, *arrivant*, as if its uncanniness had just arrived to me in a language in which it has nonetheless sounded very familiar to me for a long time.[14] The new *arrivant*, this word can, indeed, mean the neutrality of *that which* arrives, but also the singularity of *who* arrives, he or she who comes, coming to be where s/he was not expected, where one was awaiting him or her without waiting for him or her, without expecting *it* [*s'y attendre*], without knowing what or whom to expect, what or whom I am waiting for—and such is hospitality itself, hospitality toward the event. One does not expect the event of whatever, of whoever comes, arrives, and crosses the threshold—the immigrant, the emigrant, the guest, or the stranger. But if the new *arrivant* who arrives is new, one must expect—without waiting for him or her, without expecting it—that he does not simply cross a given threshold. Such an *arrivant* affects the very experience of the threshold, whose possibility he thus brings to light before one even knows whether there has been an invitation, a call, a nomination, or a promise (*Verheissung, Heissen*, etc.). What we could here call the *arrivant*, the most *arrivant* among all *arrivants*, the *arrivant* par excellence, is whatever, whoever, in arriving, does not cross a threshold separating two identifiable places, the proper and the foreign, the proper of the one and the proper of the other, as one would say that the citizen of a given identifiable country crosses the border of another country as a traveler, an emigré or a political exile, a refugee or someone who has been deported, an immigrant worker, a student or a researcher, a diplomat or a tourist. Those are all, of course, *arrivants*, but in a country that is already defined and in which the inhabitants know or think they are at home (as we saw above, this is what, according to Kant, should govern public rights, concerning both universal hospitality and visiting rights). No, I am talking about the absolute *arrivant*, who is not even a guest. He surprises the host—who is not yet a host or an inviting power—enough to call into question, to the point of annihilating or rendering indeterminate, all the distinctive signs of a prior identity, beginning with the very border that delineated a legitimate home and assured lineage, names and language, nations, families and genealogies. The absolute *arrivant* does not yet have a name or an identity. It is not an invader or an occupier, nor is it a colonizer, even if it can also become one. This is why I call it simply the *arrivant*, and not someone or something that arrives, a subject, a person, an individual, or a living thing, even less one of the migrants I just mentioned. It is not even a foreigner identified as a member of a foreign, determined community. Since the *arrivant* does not have any identity yet, its place of arrival is also de-identified: one does not yet know or one no longer knows which is the country, the place, the nation, the family, the language, and the home in general that welcomes the absolute *arrivant*. This absolute *arrivant* as such is, however, not an intruder, an invader, or a colonizer, because invasion presupposes some self-identity for the aggressor and for the victim. Nor is the *arrivant* a legislator or the discoverer of a promised land. As disarmed as a newly born child, it no more commands than is commanded by the memory of some originary event where the archaic is bound with the *final* extremity, with the finality par excellence of the *telos* or of the *eskhaton*. It even exceeds the order of any *determinable* promise. Now the border that is ultimately most difficult to delineate, because it is always already crossed, lies in the fact that the absolute *arrivant* makes possible everything to which I have just said it cannot be reduced, starting with the humanity of man, which some would be inclined to recognize in all that erases, in the *arrivant*, the characteristic of (cultural, social, or national) belonging and even metaphysical determination (ego, person, subject, consciousness, etc.). It is on this border that I am tempted to read Heidegger. Yet this border will always keep one from discriminating among the figures of the *arrivant*, the dead, and the *revenant* (the ghost, he, she, or that which returns).

If the distinction between (properly) *dying* and *perishing* cannot be reduced to a question of terminology, if it is not a linguistic distinction, for Heidegger (extending well beyond *Being and Time*) it nevertheless marks the difference *of* language, the impassable difference between the speaking being that *Dasein* is and any other living thing. *Dasein* or the mortal is not man, the human subject, but it is that in terms of which the humanity of man must be rethought. And man remains the only example of *Dasein*, as man was for Kant the only example of finite reasonable being or of *intuitus derivativus*. Heidegger never stopped modulating this affirmation according to which the mortal is whoever experiences death *as such*, as death. Since he links this possibility of the "as such" (as well as the possibility of death as such) to the possibility of speech, he thereby concludes that the animal, the living thing as such, is not properly a mortal: the animal does not relate to death as such. The animal can come to an end, that is, perish (*verenden*), it always ends up kicking the bucket [*crever*]. But it can never properly die.

Much later, in *On the Way to Language*, Heidegger wrote:

> Mortals are they who can experience death as death [*den Tod als Tod erfahren können*]. Animals cannot do this. [*Das Tier vermag dies nicht.*] But animals cannot speak either. The essential relation between death and language flashes up before us, but remains still unthought [*ist aber noch ungedacht*].[15]

It is this unthought that holds us in suspense here. For if one must assume that the difference between a mortal (whoever dies in the sense of "properly dying") and an animal incapable of dying is a certain access to death *as* death, to death *as such*, then this access will condition every distinction between these two ends, *perishing* and *dying*. By the same token, it will condition the very possibility of an analysis of *Dasein*, that is, of a distinction between *Dasein* and another mode of being, and of a distinction to which *Dasein* may *testify* by *attesting* to its proper being-able. It is therefore on the possibility of the *as such* of death that the interrogation would have to bear.

But it would also have to bear on what links the possibility of this *as such* (assuming that it can ever be assured *as such*) to the possibility or to the power of what is so obscurely called language. Indeed, Heidegger's formulation, although in some respects trenchant ("the animal is not capable of this") nevertheless retains a certain prudence. It does not say that the experience of death *as such*, the experience granted to the mortal, of which the animal is incapable, depends upon language. Heidegger says: "Animals cannot do this [experience death as death]. But animals cannot speak either. [*Das Tier kann aber auch nicht sprechen.*]" These two remarks are deliberately juxtaposed, without, however, Heidegger feeling authorized to go any further than indicating something like a flash in the sky concerning a link between the *as such* of death and language.

Therefore, several possibilities remain open:

1. There would not be any essential and irreducible link between the two, between the "as such" and language, and someone could relate to death as such *without language*, precisely where the word breaks off or defaults (*wo das Wort gebricht* or *zerbricht*, etc.). But Heidegger does not fail to recall then, as he always does, that this collapse or suspense still belongs to the possibility of language.

2. The *belief* in an experience of death *as such*, as well as the discourse crediting this belief to an experience of death *itself* and as such, would depend, on the contrary, upon an ability to speak and to name. But instead of giving us added assurance about the experience of death as death, this discourse would lose the *as such* in and through the language that would create an illusion, as if *to say*

*death* were enough to have access to dying as such—and such would be the illusion or the fantasy.

3. Consequently, since death refuses itself as such to testimony and thereby marks even what refuses its *as such* both to language and to what exceeds language, it is there that any border between the animal and the *Dasein* of speaking man would become unassignable.

4. Finally, if the living thing as such (the beast, the animal beast or human *life*, the human as living thing) is incapable of an experience of death *as such*, if, in sum, life as such does not know death as such, then this axiom will allow for a reconciliation of apparently contradictory statements, best exemplified, in my view, by the example of Heidegger, of course, but also by those of Freud and Levinas.

Once one has distinguished between these two ways of *ending*, *dying* and *perishing*, one must take into consideration what Heidegger calls an intermediate phenomenon (*Zwischenphenomenon*): the *demise*, the *Ableben*, which all the French translators agree to translate as *décès*. *Ab-leben*, to leave life, to go away from life, to walk out of life, to take a step away from life, to pass life, to trespass upon death [*trépasser*], to cross the threshold of death, thus means *de-cedere*. Already in Cicero's Latin, this figure of straying while walking signified *dying*. This reminds us that the moment of the ultimate separation, the partition that separates from life, *involves a certain step/not* [*il y va d'un certain pas*]. The French word *décès* was introduced for other reasons. Its medico-legal usage corresponds to the dominant sense of the German term *Ableben*. For the same reasons, the English translators chose to translate *Ableben* by "demise." Their footnote explains that the legalistic connotations do not, however, exhaust the meaning that Heidegger gave, in this context, to *Ableben*. What does *Ableben* (to demise) mean? It is neither dying (*Sterben*) nor perishing (*Verenden*). How does one discriminate among these three figures of ending (*enden*)? *Dasein* alone can demise (in the medico-legal sense), when it is declared dead after its so-called biological or physiological death has been certified according to conventionally accredited criteria. One does not speak of the demise of a hedgehog, of a squirrel, or of an elephant (even if, and especially if, one likes them). Demise (*Ableben*) is thus proper to *Dasein*, in any case, to what can properly die, but it is not dying (*Sterben*). *Dasein* presupposes dying, but it is not death, properly speaking: "*Dasein* never perishes [*verendet nie*]. *Dasein*, however, can demise [*ableben*] only as long as it is dying [*solange, als es stirbt*]" (p. 247).

These two sentences very economically formalize the three modes of ending (*enden*): perishing, demising, and dying. But they also bring together all of the paradoxes and chiasmi that could relate this existential analysis to what I would be tempted to locate as the two major types of concurrent discourses on death in this century, which could be identified by the names or metonymies of Freud and Levinas. In order to set up a serious discussion among these discourses, one would have to explain oneself constantly, patiently, and meticulously as to the meaning that one gives to death, and also specify which mode of *ending* one is referring to. For lack of time, let us focus on just one example.

When one keeps in mind the distinction between *verenden* and *sterben*, Heidegger's statements are not irreconcilable with the double Freudian postulate according to which there is an irreducible death drive, although neither biological *science*, nor our *belief*, nor our unconscious testifies to our mortality, an essential, necessary, or intrinsic mortality. Indeed, Heidegger says: "*Dasein nicht einfach verendet*," "*Dasein verendet nie*." Similarly, it may be enough to distinguish between *demise* and *dying* in order to avoid Levinas's objection to Heidegger regarding the originary and underivable mineness of dying. When Levinas accuses Heidegger of privileging, in the existence of *Dasein*, its proper death, what is at stake is *Sterben*. Indeed, it is in dying proper and properly speaking that "mineness" is irreplaceable, that no one can die for the other, in the experience of the hostage or of the sacrifice, in the sense of "in the place of the other," and that no testimony can testify to the contrary. But, conversely, when Levinas says and thinks that, against

Heidegger, he is saying "the death of the other is the first death" and "it is for the death of the other that I am responsible, to the point of including myself in death. This may be phrased in a more acceptable proposition: 'I am responsible for the other insofar as he is mortal,' "[16] these statements either designate the experience that I have of the death of the other in demise or they presuppose, as Heidegger does, the co-originarity of *Mitsein* and of *Sein zum Tode.* This co-originarity does not contradict, but, on the contrary, pre-supposes a mineness of dying or of being-toward-death, a mineness not that of an ego or of an egological sameness. One can also, and we will return to this later, take into consideration a sort of origi-nary mourning, something that it seems to me neither Heidegger, Freud, nor Levinas does.

Only at the end of a discussion that would have seriously taken into account this entire system of delimitations should one raise the question of how much one can trust the powerful apparatus of conceptual distinctions put forth by Heidegger. For another limit runs here. Given the theme of this conference, this limit should be of utmost importance to us. In Heidegger's view, this supplemen-tary limit not only allows one to distinguish between biological end and death properly speaking, to which the being-toward-death of *Dasein* is destined or referred. It also allows one to distinguish between all the legal, cultural, and medicoanthropological phe-nomena of demise and being-toward-death properly speaking. The distinction between demising (*Ableben*) and dying (*Sterben*) is, so to speak, *interior* to the being-toward-death of *Dasein*. Demising is not dying but, as we have seen, only a being-toward-death (*Dasein*), that is, a being-destined-to-death, a being-to-death or tending-toward-(or up-to)-death (*zum Tode*), can also *demise*. If it never perishes (*verendet nie*) as such, as *Dasein* (it can perish as living thing, animal, or man as *animal rationale,* but not as *Dasein*), if it never simply perishes (*nicht einfach verendet*), *Dasein* can nevertheless end, but therefore end without perishing (*verenden*) and without properly dying (*das Dasein aber auch enden kann, ohne daß es eigentlich stirbt*). But it cannot demise without dying. Thus, there is no scandal whatsoever in saying that *Dasein* remains immortal in its originary being-to-death, if by "immortal" one understands "without end" in the sense of *verenden*. Even if it dies (*stirbt*) and even if it *ends* (*endet*), it never "kicks the bucket" (*verendet nie*). *Dasein, Dasein* as such, does not know any end in the sense of *verenden*. At least from this angle and as *Dasein*, I am, if not immortal, then at least imperishable: I do not end, I never end, I know that I will not come to an end. And with a certain knowledge I know, *Dasein* says, that I can never perish [*je ne saurais périr*]. One should not be able to say to the other: "Kick the bucket! [*Crève!*]" (in the sense of "End!", "Perish!"). If one says it, then it takes the form of a curse and it assimilates the other into the category of animals, thereby testifying that one does not consider him an animal at the precise moment when one claims to say it to him.

This articulated set of distinctions (between perishing and dying, but also, within the existential field of *Dasein*, between death properly speaking and demise) thus presupposes *Dasein*. These delimitations also institute a hierarchy of inquiry. This hierarchy is organized around the particular kind of limit that could be called, in order to introduce a certain formalization, the *problematic closure*. The problematic closure assigns a domain, a territory, or a field to an inquiry, a research, or a knowledge. All of this is ordered in relation to a thematic object, more precisely to an entity, to a modality of the entity whose identification is presupposed by the unity of this space, which in principle can be closed. (We have been interchangeably calling such a space *fields, territories*, or *domains*, without taking into consideration, for the moment, the Kantian distinctions and the whole lexical history of the concepts of limits; this rhetoric of the space of appropriation and this space of rhetorical appropriation naturally crisscross all the themes of this conference.) We must distinguish another kind of limit from this problematic closure (and *problēma*, recall, denotes as much the task of projection as the edge of protection, the program and the shield). Let us call it the *border* [*frontière*], in what appears to be the strictest sense, that is, the sense that is statistically most common. In a way that is almost strict, if not proper, this border designates the spacing edge that, in history, and in a way that is not natural, but artificial and conventional, *nomic*, separates two national, state-controlled, linguistic, and cultural spaces. If we say that this border—in the strict or common sense—is an *anthropological* border, it is a concession to the dominant dogma according to which only man has such borders, and animals do not. One usually thinks that even if animals have territories, their territorialization (in predatory, sexual, or regular migratory drives, etc.) could not be encompassed by what man calls borders. There is nothing fortuitous about this way of thinking; this gesture denies the animal what it gives to man: death, speech, the world *as such*, the law, *and the border*. All of that would correspond to the same indissociable possibility. To these two forms of limit—the *problematic closure* and the *anthropological border*—we must also add the *conceptual demarcation* or rather the logical de-finition, that is, that which, if it were possible, would tend to oppose rigorously two concepts or the concepts of two essences, and to purify such a demarcating opposition of all contamination, of all participatory sharing, of all parasitism, and of all infection.

In a modest and preliminary way, my purpose is to investigate more closely what makes *one single braid* of these three forms of limits, to which I have given the somewhat arbitrary names of *problematic closure, anthropological border*, and *conceptual demarcation*. The aporia of death would be one of the place-names for what forms the braid and keeps it from coming undone. The analysis of a passage in Heidegger will serve here as a provisionally privileged example in order to name and draw such a braid. Let us therefore come back to §49 of *Being and Time*, which does not refer fortuitously to de-limitation; indeed, it is entitled "The Delimitation [*die Abgrenzung*] of the Existential Analysis of Death with Respect to Possible Other Interpretations of the Phenomenon." There is thus another edge between *properly dying* and the *pas* of *demise*, which already marks a double distance (with respect to death, which is left behind, but also with respect to the living thing in general, because animals, according to this hypothesis, do not demise). If it holds, this other edge would be the only one capable of separating, ordinating, superordinating, and subordinating the problematics—and that is what matters here. This edge would itself be the place of a first problematic closure, of a domain of questioning or of absolutely preliminary research. On the one hand, there would be anthropological problematics. They would take into consideration ethnologico-cultural differences affecting demise, sickness, and death; however, on the other hand, and *first of all,* there would be the ontologico-existential problematic that anthropology must presuppose and that concerns the being-until-death of *Dasein,* beyond any border, and indeed beyond any cultural, religious, linguistic, ethnological, historical, and sexual determination. In other words, there can be an anthropology or a history of death, there can be culturologies of demise, ethnologies of mortuary rites, of ritual sacrifice, of the work of mourning, of burials, of preparations for death, of the cleansing of the dead, of the languages of death in general, of medicine, and so on. But there is no culture of *death* itself or of *properly dying.* Dying is neither entirely natural (biological) nor cultural. And the question of limits articulated here is also the question of the border between cultures, languages, countries, nations, and religions, as well as that of the limit between a universal (although non-natural) structure and a differential (non-natural but cultural) structure.

# § 2 Awaiting (at)
the Arrival

All people do not die in the same way. Throughout time, they have not died in the same way. Moreover, it is not enough to recall that there are cultures of death and that from one culture to another, at the crossing of the borders, death changes face, meaning, language, or even body. "Death has changed," Philippe Ariès writes in *Essais sur l'histoire de la mort en Occident du Moyen-Age à nos jours* (p. 236). One must go further: culture itself, culture in general, is essentially, before anything, even a priori, the culture of death. Consequently, then, it is a *history of death*. There is no culture without a cult of ancestors, a ritualization of mourning and sacrifice, institutional places and modes of burial, even if they are only for the ashes of incineration. Nor is there culture without medicine, and there is no medicine without this horizon that death, so to speak, guarantees to sickness, this very singular limit called, from the Greek, "horizon." The very concept of culture may seem to be synonymous with the culture of death, as if the expression "culture of death" were ultimately a pleonasm or a tautology. But only such a redundancy can make legible the cultural difference and the grid of borders. Because every culture entails a treatise or treatment of death, each of them treats the end according to a different partition. The partition would remain at all times purely human, intra-anthropological. The difference between nature and culture, indeed between biological life and culture, and, more

43

precisely, between the animal and the human is the relation *to* death, as one most often thinks according to the same philosophical *doxa*. The relation to death *as such*. The true border would be there. Although Heidegger, deeply rooted in this tradition, repeats it, he also suggests a remarkable rearticulation of it. Forms of anthropological knowledge supposedly treat death according to culture and history; bio-genetic disciplines presumably treat death according to nature. No matter how necessary and enriching they may be, these forms of knowledge must presuppose a concept of death properly speaking—this is, in sum, what Heidegger says. Only an existential analysis can provide such a concept of death to these forms of knowledge. Heidegger describes this relation of dependence by using the classical idea of order, an order of priority, precedence, and presupposition (*vorliegen, voraussetzen*), which is also an order of foundation: there is the *founding* basis of the foundation and the *founded* structure that presupposes it. The existential interpretation of death (hence, the existential analysis of *Dasein*) "precedes" (*liegt vor*) any biology and ontology of life. It also founds (*fundiert*) any investigation of death—and Heidegger names a series: historiological, biographical, psychological, and ethnological investigations. Any "typology" of the forms of dying and of the modalities according to which demise (*Ableben*) is experienced (*erlebt*) "already presupposes the concept of death" (*setzt schon den Begriff des Todes voraus*). This "already" (*schon*) marks the time of the problematic closure: the field of anthropology (the history and the typology of the forms of demise) can only establish the markers of its problematic field by already, always already, presupposing a concept of death. The existential analysis of *Dasein* alone can provide this concept—an analysis that is not only the fundamental anthropology presupposed by it, but also the analysis of a *Dasein* that is not yet determined as human (subject, ego, conscience, person, soul, body, etc.). In order to identify the different ways of living (*erleben*) the demise (*Ableben*), that is, the ways of living as such the moment of "leaving life," the moment, in the lived experience (*Erleben*) of the living thing, of passing as a living thing, the passage out of life (*Ableben*), and in order to speak competently of these modes of passage, of the one who passes or of the other who allows the one to pass or cross, one must *already* know what *death* means, and how to recognize death properly speaking. One must *already* have an understanding or a comprehension (*Verständnis*) of what death is for *Dasein*: an understanding of the word "death" as an understanding of what relates this word to its meaning. This logic of presupposition consists in raising the question of what, already and from the outset, makes possible every statement, every determination, every theme, every project, and every object. In this context, such a logic of presupposition is also a logic of, or a request for, foundation. Indeed, Heidegger says that the existential interpretation of death precedes, is presupposed by all other discourses on death, but also founds (*fundiert*) them.

Such a request for the foundation or for the condition of possibility often speaks the language of methodology, of methodic order ("in good methodology," Heidegger says, the existential analysis comes, in terms of order, *before* biology, psychology, and other disciplines, which will be discussed in a moment; it is superordinate to them, "*methodisch vorgeordnet*," p. 248). There is a *methodological order* here in every sense of the term: (1) an order in the sense of the logic of a whole, an element, or a milieu (in the sense that one says: it is on the order of . . . ; in this case, on the order of method); (2) it is also an order as order of progression, sequence, forward motion, or irreversible procedure, a step, a way of proceeding or of progressing; (3) it is finally a given order, the double prescription to follow an order and to follow a given order of sequential linkage or of consequence: begin here and *end* there! This order of orders belongs to the great ontologico-juridico-transcendental tradition, and I believe it to be undeniable, impossible to dismantle, and invulnerable (at least this is the hypothesis that I am following here)—except perhaps in this particular case called death, which is more than a case and whose uniqueness excludes it from the system of possibilities, and specifically from the order that it, in turn, may condition. What I mean here is an entirely other "logic" of the order: if there are legitimate and powerful questions about the foundation and the "already" of the condition of possibility, then they are themselves made possible and necessary by a relation to death, by a "life-death" that no longer falls under the case of what it makes possible. That is what I will call the aporia, but we shall return to this difficulty after having followed Heidegger as far as possible.

Confident in this logic of presupposition, Heidegger would only have found confirmation, I imagine, in some of Ariès's admissions. Because Ariès did not ground his research in an ontological elucidation of what death is and signifies, he knows neither what he is talking about nor how to determine the problematic closure of his domain. In a certain way, he says so. The author of these fascinating *Essais sur l'histoire de la mort en Occident du Moyen-Age à nos jours* admits that he has not been able to delimit his field. He confesses it with an honesty that has the accent of both an always feigned and wily academic courtesy and the most disarming philosophical ingenuousness. In sum, he has never been able to assert any "border" (it is his word)—neither a cultural border (historical time and space, cultural area and periodization), nor the border that is the line crossing of death, which separates the one who is dying from the beyond of life. These two borders blur somewhat and thereby blur the borders of the very concept of death. Ariès writes:

> Every corpus was sending me to another one. [Should this be a surprise?] The first goal of my research had lost its ability to motivate me, since other, more essential problems that were taking me to the depths of being were covering it. I could guess that there were relations between the attitude before death [his real theme, which is not death itself, but behavior before demise], in its most common and general aspects, and the variations in the consciousness of the self and of the other, the sense of the individual destiny or of the large, collective fate. I was thus moving up the stream of history, happy to stumble, on this side, on a *border of culture*, the burial *ad sanctos*, the *border* of another world. I had increased the time period beyond the limits allowed by the most liberal historical usage. (p. 236, my emphasis)

There would be too much to say, in the time that we have here, about the methodological or theoretico-metaphysical axioms that govern Ariès's work. And to point out the limits of these axioms and the limit of his thought about limits is not to denigrate the interest of his work. Consider, for example, his article "Collective Unconscious and Clear Ideas" (in *Essais*, pp. 236–37), in which, in a way that is both interesting and disappointing, Ariès again discusses the "border" and the "limit" (his terms). This time, not only the limit between the biological and the cultural is in question, but also "classificatory hypotheses" and what is calmly called a "theoretical and speculative problem!", with an exclamation mark, and put off for later:

> I tend to underestimate the influence of religious and cultural systems: neither the Renaissance nor the Enlightenment appears as a decisive landmark in my periodization. The Church interests me more insofar as it indicates and reveals unnoticed feelings than as a pressure group that would have governed feelings at their sources. According to me, the large drifting movements that put beliefs and attitudes into motion—attitudes before life and death—depend on more secret, more hidden motors, at the limit of the biological and the cultural, that is, at the limit of the "*collective unconscious.*" [The term is underlined by Ariès, who thinks that here he can use all these terms and concepts—beliefs, attitudes, life, death, limit, biological and cultural, collective unconscious—as if their intelligibility was guaranteed and did not cover up abysses or, if the historian finds the following hypothesis more reassuring, did not cover up mountains of archives that up to this day and for some time still to come have not been classified and are unclassifiable.] It animates elementary psychological forces, such as self-consciousness, desire to be more, or, on the contrary, sense of collective fate, sociability, and so on.

Then, alluding to a debate that opposes him to Michel Vovelle, the other well-known historian of death:

> Vovelle also acknowledges the importance of the collective unconscious, but, as he has shown in his remarkable *Mourir autrefois* [Dying in other times], he tends to put more weight on customs than I have

granted to what we have called, in our all-too-short debate, clear ideas: religious doctrines, political and moral philosophies, psychological effects of scientific and technical progress, and socio-economic systems. . . . We have only been able to show that there was a problem: a problem that may appear to be theoretical or speculative!

After that, although he does not draw any consequence from this in his work, Ariès in sum acknowledges and confirms in his own way what Heidegger says about what conditions and determines knowledge and historical research (or anthropological research in general):

> In fact, it ["the theoretical or speculative problem!"] determines the historian's practice, for how is it possible to distinguish things and then to organize them without a classificatory hypothesis? And how is it possible to establish such an overall conception, whether it is acknowledged or not? (All quotes are from p. 237).

This "overall conception" obscurely predetermines at least two things. (1) On the one hand, it predetermines everything that stems from the delimitation of the problematic field: Is this "history"? (history of what?) of "ideas and attitudes," as is said? (what are those?), of the "collective unconscious"? (what is that?), of "self-consciousness"? (what is that?), of the "effects" (on social practices, of science and technology? is this psychoanalysis? psychoanalysis of what?) (2) On the other hand, in the hypothesis where it would be history, and since it presents itself under this name, this so-called "overall conception" obscurely, and in a blurred or blurring way, predetermines the intra-historical delimitations, that is, the periodization with which Ariès admits having difficulty, even though he is more modest than Thomas and limits himself to the Christian West from the Middle Ages to the present. Recall that he admits having a lot of difficulty with certain borders of periodization, but in fact his difficulties are much greater than he admits. Sometimes he warns against anachronism (for example, *Essais*, p. 17), but on a number of occasions he must mention "anachronistic" occurrences, that is, significant occurrences that do not belong to the time within which the historian both thinks he can inscribe them and assumes that they can be inscribed. One even has the impression that a certain anachronism is the rule with respect to these delimitations. "Life will have been so short": this means that one always dies in an untimely way [*à contretemps*]. The moment of death no longer belongs to its time [*son temps*], at least by a certain aspect that, nonetheless, does not fail to historicize itself and perhaps provide the occasion of the history with which historians deal. One should ask why this anachronism insists with respect to death. In particular, I refer to what Ariès judges to be "close to modern eroticism" (p. 85), even though it happened before modernity, and also to what describes "The death of the libertine," which is the title of a chapter in *L'Homme devant la mort* (II: 24–25). Discussing arts of dying, which are as much, and indeed first of all, ways of living (such as Bellarmin's *de arte bene moriendi*), Ariès insists upon the recurrence of ideas that *announce* the Enlightenment before the Enlightenment and that, no matter how "anachronistic" or "exceptional" they may seem, are nonetheless recurrent, "verified and confirmed" by testimonies. In order not to multiply the examples, I am thinking above all of Sade's extraordinary will. It would deserve an analysis that I must unfortunately leave aside. This will, "written with seriousness and conviction," Ariès notes, is defined by the historian as "both utopian for the eighteenth century and already anachronistic for the year 1806" (What is this category, the "already anachronistic"?) It is "utopian" and "already anachronistic" because it "testifies to a complete confusion of two opinions that were up to then close to one another, but separate: the contempt for the body and the radical refusal of immortality." Faced with the internal contradictions of this will which, as Ariès himself notes, requests both that one monumentalize the traces of the effacement that it calls for and that one carry out a ceremony of the absence of ceremony, the historian never wonders whether the anachronism and the internal aporia of this may not signify something other than just the untimeliness of an eccentric who is mistaken about the time he lives in.[17]

As Thomas will also do, just as he dismissed the "theoretical," the "speculative," or the "overall conception," Ariès does not hesitate to call "metaphysical" everything that the historian must respectfully leave aside and assume accessible to common sense or universal experience. *Metaphysical, the metaphysical nature of death*: such would be the "deepest reason" for the problems of limits and borders encountered by the historian. But instead of asking himself what "metaphysical" means here and without stopping at these "deep reasons," Ariès courageously pursues his inquiry and describes what he dares to call the "slowness of his progression," namely, the fact that he devoted "fifteen years" to this task. Fifteen years! Fifteen years seem enormous to the historian for writing a history of death in the West from the Middle Ages to the present; according to him, this slowness is ultimately explained by the metaphysical obscurity of death, by the "*metaphysical* nature of death":

> It may be surprising that it took me so long to arrive here: fifteen years of research and meditation on the attitudes before death in our Western Christian cultures! The slowness of my progression must not be attributed only to material obstacles, to a lack of time, or to a weariness in front of the immensity of the task. There is another, deeper reason, which has to do with the *metaphysical* nature of death: the field of my research moved backward when I thought I was reaching its limits, and I was each time pushed further, both upstream and downstream in relation to my starting point (p. 12).

Why underline Ariès's term "metaphysical"? At least he should be credited for not citing Heidegger, whereas, we recall, Thomas wildly attributes to Heidegger what he calls the "metaphysical truth" of a sentence that is not even Heidegger's. Let us return briefly to the Heideggerian delimitation of problematic closures. What disciplines or problematics, according to Heidegger, do not elucidate their presupposed foundations, the very foundations of which the existential analysis of death must remind them? They include not only the anthropological sciences, ethnology, psychology, history—in short all the theories dealing with a culture of death. Metaphysics and theology are also included there. Indeed, for methodological reasons, Heidegger distinguishes the existential analysis of death, which legitimately comes first, from *any other* discourse on death—discourses from biological or anthropological disciplines, to be sure, but also from metaphysics or theology. With respect to all these problematics, the existential analysis is both anterior and free, first and neutral. Anthropological knowledge can be psychologies or ethnologies of death. In the best hypothesis, psychology (and Heidegger would probably include here psycho-analysis, rightly or wrongly) can be a psychology of *the dying*, hence of *the living*, of whoever is still on this side of death, rather than a discourse on dying. (What Heidegger then notes could easily turn itself against the existential analysis of death. *Dasein* cannot *testify* to death either; it is also as one living or dying that it attests to being-for-death.) At that point, it remains that, in Heidegger's view, if so-called psychology remains a psychology of life, that is, of the dying rather than of dying, this merely reflects, like a reflection (*Widerschein*), the fact that *Dasein* does not die or does not prop-erly die (*nicht eigentlich stirbt*) in the course of an experience, of a living, or of a lived experience as one sometimes says somewhat ridiculously in order to translate *Erleben, Erlebnis*. *Dasein* never has the *Erleben* of its own demise (*Ableben*), or of its own death (*Sterben*). This, however, does not mean that it cannot *testify*, according to a concept of testimony (*Bezeugung*) that should be questioned here because it plays a major role in *Being and Time* and because it is neither simply phenomenological nor free of all phe-nomenology, at least if *Erlebnis* is the measure of the phenomeno-logical.

According to a similar outline, what holds for psychology, psy-choanalysis, even phenomenological psychology also holds for eth-nology, a discipline specializing in the study of the cultural borders separating the relation to death, to murder, to the sacrifice of life, to mourning, and to burial. Heidegger devotes only one sentence to it, in a paragraph that returns to the presuppositions, and therefore to the problematic closure, of any "typology" of "dying." After having mentioned just as briefly the psychology of the dying, he notes that the same holds for the study of the relation to death "among primitive peoples" (*bei den Primitiven*), and also for the study of their attitudes, magic, and cults. This primarily (*primär*) sheds light on the fact that the primitives in question have access to *Dasein*, to death for *Dasein*, and to an understanding of *Dasein* (*Daseinsverständnis*) that also requires, therefore, an existential analysis and a concept that corresponds to this understanding. There is therefore no limit to the universality of this analysis. Even if one considered it as an anthropology, which it is not, at least it would be in this respect general or fundamental, because it is universal.

The same problematic closure and therefore the same methodological presuppositions concern the "metaphysics of death" (*Metaphysik des Todes*). The existential analysis of death is also anterior, neutral, and independent with regard to all the questions and all the answers pertaining to a metaphysics of death: the questions and answers that concern survival, immortality, the beyond (*das Jenseits*), or the other side of this side (*das Diesseits*), that is, what one should do or think *down here* before death (ethical, juridical, and political norms). Since this figure of the border and of the line between the here and the beyond [*l'en-deçà et l'au-delà*] is of particular interest to us here, we should note that, after having excluded from the existential analysis all considerations about the beyond and the here (the "on this side," *das Diesseits*, which must not be translated by the Platonic or Christian "down here"), arguing that they are founded, dependent, and derivative with regard to the existential analysis, Heidegger nevertheless stresses that the existential analysis stands, not in "immanence," as Martineau, losing the thread, writes in his translation, but purely on this side: it is *rein "diesseitig."* It is on this side, on the side of *Dasein* and of its here, which is our here, that the oppositions between here and over there, this side and beyond, can be distinguished. In the same direction, one could say that it is by always *starting from* the idiomatic hereness of my language, my culture, and my belongings that I relate myself to the difference of the over there. To wonder what there is after death only has meaning and is legitimately possible (*mit Sinn und Recht*)—it is only "methodologically certain" (*methodisch sicher*: Heidegger rarely claims methodological order and derivative legitimacy as often as in these pages)—if one has elaborated a concept of the ontological essence of death and if one remembers that the possibility of being of every *Dasein* is engaged, invested, and inscribed in the phenomenon of death (*in dieses hereinsteht*). I do not have time to discuss further this methodologism, which poses as its axiom that one can only *start* from *here*, from *this side*: the best point of departure is the point from which we can start and that is always here. Where does one start from, if not from here? Such is the thrust of a question that may not be as invincible as it looks. This question can be addressed to the same axiomatic that, at the beginning of *Being and Time* (§§2, 3, and 4), justifies "the ontico-ontological priority [*Der ontisch-ontologische Vorrang*]" of *Dasein*, the "exemplary" point of departure of the existential analysis in *Dasein*, as *this* particular power of questioning that *we* are, we *here*, we who can pre-understand being, comprehend it pre-ontologically, wait for each other [*nous attendre*], expect [*nous attendre-à*], listen to and understand each other [*nous entendre*]. Concerning the existential analysis of death (§49), the same decision characterizes the point of departure: the decision is taken *here*. Heidegger's determination seems to be both decisive, that is to say, incisive, taking itself to be immediately justified by the very fact that the decision is made *here* concerning the *here*, and nonetheless rather anxious. Indeed, Heidegger allows something undecided to remain suspended as to whether the point of departure is "on this side" and not on that side of a possible border. For, perhaps in a form of avowal, he then declares: "Whether such a question is a possible *theoretical* question [*theoretische* is underlined] at all must remain undecided here [*bleibe hier unentschieden*]." He does not use the indicative: this remains undecided (*bleibt unentschieden*). Instead, by another decision whose performative incision must remain still undisputable and undisputed (let us rather say, irrecusable or uncontested, for what is involved is a matter of testimony and not of proof), he uses the subjunctive: "that it remain undecided, must remain undecided" (subjunctive, *bleibe unentschieden*, and "here," *bleibe hier unentschieden*). The theoretical question concerning the here, the "this side" as point of departure *must* remain *here, on this side*, undecided, that is to say, decided without any theoretical question, before any theoretical question: without proof. It must remain this way because one cannot do otherwise, it is necessary; and it must remain this way because, as soon as one cannot do otherwise, one must do it this way, it is better to do it this way: *here, in any case.* The theoretical question can only be raised afterwards, and its nature can only be speculative, not phenomenological. Such is the authoritative conclusion of the paragraph: "Die diesseitige ontologische Interpretation des Todes liegt vor jeder ontisch-jenseitigen Spekulation"; "insofar as it operates on this side [*citra, intra,* on this side of the border: *diesseitige*] the ontological interpretation of death precedes all ontical speculation operating beyond, on the other side [as *ultra, meta, trans*]."

It is impossible to overemphasize the importance of what is *being decided,* so authoritatively and so decisively, at the very moment when what is in question is to decide on what *must remain undecided.* Its signification seems to be decisive precisely with regard to all the borders that we are discussing. For at least *three reasons.*

1. On the one hand, there is no limit to the effects of a decision that, presenting itself as "methodological," organizes and hierarchizes all the delimitations that have here been called problematic closures. It extends to all problematics, all disciplines, and all forms of knowledge about death. "Methodologically, the existential analysis is superordinate [*ist methodisch vorgeordnet*] to the problematic [or the questioning: *den Fragen*] of a biology, psychology, theodicy, or theology of death" (p. 248). Of course, since it thus precedes all content of knowledge, such an analysis may seem to be formal and empty, at least from the viewpoint of an ontical content, for any ontology then seems formal and empty. Heidegger recognizes this, but he sees here only an appearance, which should not blind us to the differentiated richness of the phenomenal structures described by such an analysis. Later, we will raise the question of whether, in order to sustain this existential analysis, the so-called ontological content does not surreptitiously reintroduce, in the mode of ontological repetition, theorems and theologemes pertaining to disci-

plines that are said to be founded and dependent—among others, Judeo-Christian theology, but also all the anthropologies that are rooted there.

2. On the other hand, it is not enough to say that Heidegger interprets death in terms of a decision that consists in privileging the "this side" (*das Diesseits*) of the line, even if at the same time he neutralizes the interest for the other side of a beyond that would be opposed to this side. Rather, it seems to me that one should say the opposite: it is the originary and underivable character of death, as well as the finitude of the temporality in which death is rooted, that decides and forces us to decide to start from here first, from this side here. A mortal can only start from here, from his mortality. His possible belief in immortality, his irresistible interest in the beyond, in gods or spirits, what makes survival structure every instant in a kind of irreducible torsion, the torsion of a retrospective anticipation that introduces the untimely moment and the posthumous in the most alive of the present living thing, the rearview mirror of a waiting-for-death [*s'attendre-à-la mort*] at every moment, and the future anterior that precedes even the present, which it only seems to modify, all this stems first from his mortality, Heidegger would say. No matter how serious all this remains, it would thus only be secondary. This very secondariness testifies to the primordiality of being-toward-death, of being-until-death, or, as one could also say, of being-to-death. Only a being-to-death can think, desire, project, indeed, "live" immortality *as such*. (Here there is an affirmation of originary finitude that Hegel thought he had reversed in Kant, not without good reason: one cannot think originary finitude without removing it as infinity, nor can one think being-to-death without starting from immortality. As is most often the case, here Heidegger is on Kant's side, on *this side* of finitude, and not on Hegel's side. But is not Hegel the one who wanted to think the unilaterality of the border and thereby show that one is always already on the other side of the here? Let us leave this enormous question in parentheses.) The theme of immortality, like that of any form of survival or return [*revenance*] (and society, culture, memory, spirit, and

spirits are made only of that—only for that) is not opposed to being-toward-death, it does not contradict it, it is not symmetrical with it, because it is conditioned by being-toward-death and confirms it at every moment. The incontestability of being-toward-death, the non-derivation of certainty concerning being-toward-death (at least as Heidegger will assert it), would not leave any other methodologically rigorous choice than that of starting from "this side."

3. And finally, if it is *incontestable* (who could testify against it? and from where?), the prevalence of "this side" is also, in this analysis, a certain prevalence of the phenomenological tradition. It goes *hand in hand*—and this is an absolute indissociability—with everything that, in existential analysis, becomes prevalence itself, not a prevalence or hierarchizing valorization among others, but rather the prevailing of every evaluation and every possible hierarchy, the *pre*-ferring of *pre*-ferance [*pré-férance*, with an "a"] itself, that is, the pre-archic originarity of the proper, the authentic, and the *eigentlich*.

Before getting to it as to the ultimate aporia, let me indicate, at least schematically and for the record, a few corollaries. The decision to decide from the *here* of this side is not simply a methodological decision, because it decides upon the very method: it decides that a method is pre-ferable, and better, than a non-method. It is not surprising to see this absolute decision turn into a non-decision, since it is an unconditional decision concerning the place and the taking-place of the decision. In fact, it is not even, not yet, or already no longer a decision because, on the one hand, it relies on a prevalence rooted in precisely what cannot be decided, that is, in death, and, on the other hand and for that very reason, it leaves undecided (*unentscheidet*) the theoretico-speculative questions that could impose themselves, the questions that would make one hesitate between decision and non-decision, as between the two poles of one alternative. (One could perhaps conclude from this that the essence of decision, i.e., what would make decision be the object of thematic knowledge or of theoretical discourse, must remain undecidable in order for there to be decision, if there is such a thing.)

What are these corollaries? Let us stick with those that intersect with the themes of our conference.

I. FIRST COROLLARY: *death would have no border.* The only consistent way of attempting to ground a really universal discourse is no doubt to grant the existential analysis of death priority and absolute independence with regard to any other problematic, discipline, research, and region. Then, existential structures no longer depend upon any given anthropological culture; they do not stop at the vision of the world, the language, or the religion of any particular society, European or not; they do not stop at any sexual difference. The existential analysis of *Dasein* would ultimately be the only discipline for which death does not know any border. No historical limit and no periodization would affect its principle. Heidegger's analyses would thus exceed and implicitly condition both a history of the type that Ariès suggests (a history of death in the West, in the Christian West, from the Middle Ages to the present) as well as an "anthropo-thanatology" such as Thomas's, which claims to be "comparative" ("any anthropology of death can only be comparative," p. 531). Moreover, beyond their supposedly theoretical and constative knowledge, the anthropological historian and the comparatist anthropo-thanatologian multiply cultural and political evaluations. They both *deplore* and *denounce* what, according to them, they must record: a sort of disappearance of death in the modern West and in industrialized societies. They even *declare* their disapproval and denunciation, they put it forth, they recognize therein a determinant motivation of their research. For us, in the West, within our borders, death would be, and increasingly so, almost prohibited, dissimulated, disposed of, and denied. "The prohibitions of death," Ariès writes, "born in the United States and in northwestern Europe during the twentieth century, penetrated into France from then on" (p. 15). An affirmation just as massive and careless can also be found in Thomas, inspiring him with an admiring nostalgia for the model of an Africa that he calls "traditional." According to Thomas, Africa "offers [us] a remarkable example of how the problems of death are resolved, an example that probably exists in other non-industrialized populations, and which may have existed in the European past" (p. 531). Indeed, Thomas wants *to resolve* the problem of death, nothing more and nothing less. Like Dali, up to the end he will probably think that "it will all work out." Deploring the fact that the industrial West wants to deny or hold death at a distance, Thomas suggests that one should know death better so as to "put it back into its rightful place": "To know death better is *to put it back into its rightful place* [the author underlines this incredible expression] by avoiding at once the refusal to take it into consideration (denial), the obsessional fascination that makes us lose sight of the battle for a better life, and the evasion toward fantasies of consolation (narcissism) or compensation (mortifying behavior)" (p. 534).

The existential analysis maintains itself well this side of all this foolish comparatist predication, even if, at its root, and we will surely return to this, a judgment on the loss of authenticity in the relation to death also reveals, in its way—in Heidegger's way—a certain incapacity to look death in the face, to assume in a resolute fashion being-toward-death, a certain everyday leveling that is not always foreign to what is being exacerbated by a certain modernity of the modern industrial city. In short, across all these differences, the dominant feeling for everyone is that death, you see, is no longer what it used to be. And who will deny it?

And who would not recognize here the crossing of borders? For, if death figures this theme or this fundamental concept, which guarantees the very possibility of the existential analysis, it is also and first of all because death takes a figure. It has a privileged form, the crossing of a line (between existence and non-existence, *Dasein* and non-*Dasein*—I am not saying between living and dying). Upon this figure depend all the threads of the braid mentioned above:

1. The thread that passes between two cultural or historical *borders* (being-to-death would here be without border, hence universal, but universal within the borders that separate *Dasein*

from any other entity and from any other living thing, in particular from the animal);

2. the thread between two *problematic closures* (the difference between the existential analysis of death and any other regional knowledge or general discipline of death);

3. finally, the thread that follows the line of logical *demarcation* among all the concepts pertaining to these problematics.

2. SECOND COROLLARY: *a politics of death.* If the existential analysis of death wants to be at the same time primary and universal (although Heidegger does not use this word, which has connotations that are too humanistic, too formal, and too dependent upon a certain *Aufklärung*), and if it claims to remain neutral with regard to culture, morality, theology, and metaphysics, it must obviously also be so with regard to all politics. There is no politics of death—of death *properly speaking.* The existential analysis does not claim any competence (and indeed, it has none) for dealing with political problems of burial, of the cult of the dead, and, above all, of war and of medicine. True, historical anthropologies do not have much to say either on this subject, particularly on the most original forms that it can take today. Think for example of the hostage war, which seems to be (but is this certain?) one of the irreducible givens of modernity (and in particular of technical modernity and of its treatment of speed: modes of transportation [aviation] and of communication [telephone, mass media, television, etc.]). Insofar as it depends upon this technical modernity, the hostage war also presupposes a massive economico-cultural heterogeneity among several experiences of the relation to death, to the individual's mortality, and to his place in society. A given society cannot treat its individual subjects in the same way as another society can. One can do no more here than recall, without exaggerated *pathos*, the space of a politics of death or of mass extermination, the developments of a modern hostage war that probably began with kidnapping (there cannot be any kidnapping, in the strict sense, without automobiles, without a certain condition of posts, telephones, and telecommunications, for example), then developed in Europe under Nazism,

and has recently expanded to worldwide dimensions. The difference in the treatment of individual or mass death has consequences for modern war: it is not in the same way, even if it is called surgical, that one bombards Iraq and Sarajevo in the name of international law; and the disproportion in the evaluation of the enemies' deaths continues to change constantly, just as "dying for one's country" has changed. The same mutation has transformed medicine and modern bio-genetics. In every sense of the word "to treat," one does not treat AIDS in industrial European societies as one treats it, without treating it, in Africa; one does not even treat the statistics of AIDS in the same way. And the progress of research on the so-called human genome (data banks, predictive medicine—thus for the moment still not covered by health insurance—which could not, at least easily, be transferred to developing countries) will drastically exacerbate the differences between the rich and the less rich in our societies, and even more so between our countries and poor countries. They will do so with respect to life and death, to sickness and socio-medical insurance, and to all the givens of what one calls bioethics, which by the same token is also a thanato-ethics—and a thanato-ethics is necessarily a general euthanato-ethics, a philosophy of euthanasia and of dying well, in general (*ars de bene moriendi*). One must indeed die and die well [*Il faut bien mourir*].

In fact, if not by right, and like the anthropo-thanatologies mentioned above, the existential analysis of death has nothing to say on this matter that is not its subject. At least this is what the existential analysis says, for it is not certain that Heidegger does not ultimately give us a discourse on *the best*, indeed *the most proper and the most authentic*, relation to dying: hence, *de bene moriendi*.

3. The THIRD COROLLARY can also be political: it is what would make us pass, in spirit, from the hostage to the host/guest and from the host/guest to the ghost. (This is the series constituted by hostage, host, guest, ghost, holy ghost, and *Geist*.) In *Being and Time*, the existential analysis does not want to know anything about the ghost [*revenant*] or about mourning. Everything that can be said about them, as interesting as it may sometimes sound,

would certainly stem, in Heidegger's view, from derivative disciplines such as psychology or psychoanalysis, theology or metaphysics. It would concern the figures or the experiences of demise
(*Ableben*) rather than death properly speaking. Such would be his
fast answer (too fast for me) to whoever would be tempted to
consider mourning and ghosting [*revenance*], spectrality or living-
on, surviving, as non-derivable categories or as non-reducible deri-
vations (non-reducible to the fundamental debate in which I said
that Freud, Heidegger, and Levinas make up the three most determinant angles). If *Jemeinigkeit*, that of *Dasein* or that of the ego (in
the common sense, the psychoanalytic sense, or Levinas's sense) is
constituted in its ipseity in terms of an originary mourning, then
this self-relation welcomes or supposes the other within its being-
itself as different from itself. And reciprocally: the relation to the
other (in itself outside myself, outside myself in myself) will never
be distinguishable from a bereaved apprehension. The relevance of
the question of knowing whether it is from one's own proper death
or from the other's death that the relation to death or the certitude
of death is instituted is thus limited from the start. Even where one
speaks of *Jemeinigkeit*, these limits would be those of the *ego* and
sometimes simply those of the conscious "I" and of that to which it
thinks it can *testify*. Whoever tries, as I would like to do, to draw the
necessary consequences (they are incalculably numerous; they are
the incalculable itself), would find himself accused of still presupposing the existential analysis of *Dasein* at the very moment when
he would, on the contrary, claim to extract its presuppositions or to
extract himself from its presupposed axioms. But since the recipro-
cal axiom would also be necessary, let us leave this corollary suspended. Although everything is, to a certain extent, tied to this
corollary, I shall simply point out that it also includes a political
dimension. It may even engage the political in its essence. In an
economic, elliptic, hence dogmatic way, I would say that there is no
politics without an organization of the time and space of mourning, without a topolitology of the sepulcher, without an anamnesic
and thematic relation to the spirit as ghost [*revenant*], without an
open hospitality to the guest as *ghost* [in English in the original],

whom one holds, just as he holds us, hostage. In this regard, one could extend beyond the limits that he ascribes to it, namely, a discourse on "primitives," a remark of Valéry that I recently came upon in his Preface to Sir James Frazer's *La Crainte des morts* (Paris, 1934). Speaking of "the ancient belief *that the dead are not dead*, or *are not quite dead*," Valéry defines Frazer's project in the following manner: "to represent for us, with numerous examples, what one could call the Politics of the Primitives in their relations with the spirits of the dead." These fascinating "numerous examples" always describe a crossing *of* borders: of the border that separates the world of the living from that of the dead, of course, but as soon as the crossing goes in both directions, hin and fro, the same border is more or less than one, and more or less than one from one culture to another.

I am, here, now, reaching the end. If possible.

The concept of *possibility* will allow me, legitimately or not, to weave a certain number of motifs into the existential analysis of death, as it is carried out in *Being and Time*. The only rule would be that of a title and what accompanies it (*Aporias*, Dying—awaiting (one another at) "the limits of truth" [*S'attendre aux "limites de la vérité"*]) at the point where it subscribes to the contract of this conference.

A certain thinking of the *possible* is at the heart of the existential analysis of death. (For Heidegger, moreover, it is never very far from the thinking of the heart.) This possibility of the possible brings together *on the one hand* the sense of the virtuality or of the imminence of the future, of the "that can always happen at any instant," one *must expect it, I am expecting it, we are expecting it,* and *on the other hand,* the sense of ability, of the possible as that of which I am capable, that for which I have the power, the ability, or the potentiality. These two meanings of possibility co-exist in *die Möglichkeit.* At the end of this "*Abgrenzung* (of the Existential Analysis of Death with Respect to Possible Other Interpretations)" (§49), hence with respect to what we have called the other problematic closures, Heidegger suggests a sort of diagnosis. Remarking upon the insufficiency of all these problematics, this diagnosis therefore traces a general line of delimitation. These problematics neglect, forget, and misrecognize the essence of *Dasein*. *Dasein* is not an entity that is here in front of me or that I can put my hands on, like a substantial object, *als Vorhandenes*. Instead, the essence of *Dasein* as entity is precisely the *possibility*, the being-possible (*das Möglichsein*). In other words, because they exclude or do not recognize this strange dimension of the possible, all these problematic closures lock *Dasein* into an ontological determination that is not its own, that of the *Vorhandensein*. And if they lock it up, that is already in order to give in to a confusion between death and an end leveled by the average, mediocre, and leveling everydayness of *Dasein*. This confusion leads to speaking nonsense; it leads all these bio- or thanato-anthropo-theological problematics toward arbitrariness. In order to avoid this arbitrariness, one must come back to an ontological determination of the kind of being that *Dasein* is and to an ontological determination of the limit that separates *Dasein* from *Vorhandensein* and from *Zuhandensein*. In this way, to put it in a word and all too quickly, if the limit that passes between these three types of entity, *Dasein*, *Zuhandensein*, and *Vorhandensein*, was not guaranteed (as I have tried elsewhere to suggest is the case, particularly in "The Hand of Heidegger"), then this whole discourse on death would risk losing something of its fundamentality (but I leave this argument aside for the moment because it relates to our subject in too mediated a way).

If being-possible is the being proper to *Dasein*, then the existential analysis of the death of *Dasein* will have to make of this *possibility* its theme. Like an example, the analysis of death is submitted to the ontological law that rules the being of *Dasein*, whose name is "possibility." But death is possibility par excellence. Death exemplarily guides the existential analysis. And this is precisely what happens in the pages that immediately follow the delimitation (*die Abgrenzung*).

It is therefore necessary to isolate *two typical series of ontological statements* concerning possibility. They are articulated with each other; they supplement and engender each other, like the two moments of a single aporetic sentence.

The first statements are assertions and characterize death as *Dasein*'s most proper possibility. Being-possible is proper to *Dasein* as entity, and death is the most proper possibility of this possibility. This typical statement distributes itself, modulates itself, and is argued in many ways, but its recurrency gives its rhythm to the entire ending of the chapter, that is, the four long paragraphs or subchapters (§§50–53). This possibility of being is not a simple characteristic to be noted or described. In its essential and constant imminence, it must be *assumed*; one can and one must testify to it; and the testimony is not a mere constative report: the statements of the existential analysis are originarily prescriptive or normative. More precisely, they analyze an irreducible prescriptivity, which itself stems from being as being-possible, but they do so in the mode of phenomenological attestation (this is the considerable problem of *Bezeugung* that I signaled too quickly above): "Death is a possibility-of-being that Dasein itself has to take over [*zu über-nehmen*] in every case. With death, Dasein awaits itself [*s'at-tend lui-même, steht sich . . . bevor,* "stands before" in Macquarrie and Robinson] in its ownmost potentiality-for-being" (p. 250).

What am I translating here, in a slightly strange way, by "awaits itself" [*s'at-tendre*]? In the French grammatical construction *s'at-tendre*, where the untranslatability of the idiom can produce effects of shibboleth, several transitivities intersect and proliferate. One, not very common, seems to be a reflexive construction with no object properly speaking, with no other object toward which to tend than oneself. (One simply awaits oneself [*on s'attend soi-même*]: I await myself, and nothing else; I myself await myself in myself; and this is the most identifiable and most identifying self-relation, i.e., the ego's memory or promise of itself.) The other syntax of transitivity relates *to* [à] something, indeed, *to* something completely other: one is expecting [on s'attend *à*]—and my subtitle (*Mourir—s'attendre aux "limites de la vérité"*) leaves this instability in movement: to expect the limits [*s'attendre aux limites*], to expect meeting the limits [*s'attendre à rencontrer les limites*] *and* to await oneself at the limits [*s'attendre soi-même aux limites*], to have a meeting with oneself in this place, in these parts [*parages*] that one calls the "limits of truth," in the vicinity of these limits. But this instability can even lead us elsewhere, and in truth can lead us to the limits from which the instability itself proceeds, at the very origin of the destabilizing movement.

How? First, let us summarize. One thus can: (1) Await oneself, await oneself in oneself. (2) As long as the waiting can only be directed toward some other and toward some *arrivant*, one can and must wait for something else, hence expect some other—as when one is said to expect *that* something will happen or that some other will arrive. In both cases the *awaiting oneself* [le s'attendre soi-même] and the *expecting* [le s'attendre-à] or the *expecting-that* [le s'attendre-que] can have a notable relation to death, to what is called—death (it is there, and maybe only there, that one ultimately *awaits oneself* or *expects*, that one *expects that*; and it is only there that the *awaiting oneself* may be no other than the *expecting the other, or that* the other may arrive). (3) But there is a third and maybe first possibility in this grammatical structure: we can wait for each other [*s'attendre l'un l'autre, l'une l'autre*], and not only is the reflexive construction of the absolute awaiting *each other* [*s'attendre*] not incompatible, but in fact, it is immediately consonant with the most heterological reference to the completely other. This reference is more heterological than ever—others would say as close as ever to the limits of truth—when the waiting for *each other* is related to death, to the borders of death, where we wait for each other knowing *a priori*, and absolutely undeniably, that, life always being too short, the one is waiting for the other there, for the one and the other never arrive there together, at this rendezvous (death is ultimately the name of impossible simultaneity and of an impossibility that we know simultaneously, at which we await each other, at the same time, *ama* as one says in Greek: at the same time, simultaneously, we are expecting this anachronism and this contretemps). Both the one and the other never arrive together at this rendezvous, and the one who waits for the other there, at this border, is not he who arrives there first or she who gets there first. In order to wait for the other at this meeting place, one must, on the contrary, arrive there late, not early. Taking into consideration the anachronism of the waiting for each other in this contretemps of mourning would certainly change the commonly and hastily assumed premises of the triangular debate that we assigned to Freud, Heidegger, and Levinas: with respect to death, the death of oneself, and the death of the other.

The *s'attendre* that I have used in order to translate Heidegger's sentence involves imminence, indeed, the anxious anticipation of something, but also the double or rather triple transitivity (nonreflexive and reflexive) of the expecting, the waiting for *something* that will happen as the completely other than oneself, but of waiting (for each other) by awaiting oneself also [*s'attendre en s'attendant du même coup soi-même*], by preceding oneself as if one had a meeting with a oneself that one is but does not know. The German sentence says, "Mit dem Tod steht sich das Dasein selbst in seinem eigensten Seinkönnen bevor." Martineau translates *steht bevor* by *se pré-cède* [precedes itself] ("Avec la mort, le *Dasein* se précède lui-même en son pouvoir-être le plus propre"; with death Dasein pre-cedes itself in its most proper being-able). Vezen translates *steht bevor* by *a rendez-vous*, has a rendezvous ("Avec la mort le *Dasein* a rendez-vous avec lui-même dans son pouvoir être le plus propre"; with death Dasein has a rendezvous with itself in its most proper being-able). Macquarrie and Robinson remind us of another connotation of being-before-itself when they translate it more literally by "stands before itself" ("With death, Dasein stands before itself in its ownmost potentiality for being"). With death, *Dasein* is indeed *in front of* itself, *before* itself (*bevor*), both as before a mirror and as before the future: it awaits itself [*s'attend*], it precedes itself [*se précède*], it has a rendezvous with itself. *Dasein* stretches [*se tend*], bends *toward* [*se tend vers*] its most proper being-able, offers to itself [*se tend*] its most proper being-able; it offers it to itself [*se le tend*] as much as it bends toward it [*tend vers lui*], as soon as the latter is nothing other than itself. What is most important is this *in seinem eigensten Seinkönnen*—and Heidegger underlines the *eigensten*, the most proper. Further on, he repeats the same expression, and he underlines it again a little later, near the word *Bevorstand*, which echoes *steht bevor*: "So enthüllt sich der *Tod* als die *eigenste, unbezügliche*, unüberholbare Möglichkeit. Als solche ist er eine *ausgezeichneter* Bevorstand"; "Thus death unveils itself as the most proper, absolute (absolutely non-relational), possibility, a possibility that is not to be outstripped. As such, death is something *distinctively* impending [*l'imminence insigne du s'attendre*]" (pp. 250–51). The self-unveiling (*So enthüllt sich der Tod*) bespeaks a truth of death, indeed a truth as truth of death whose internal limit we shall return to soon. The definition of death as the most proper possibility comes back insistently and in the same terms in §51 (p. 255) and in §52 (pp. 259–60), in order to describe both the anxiety that must be related to this most proper possibility and the fear that keeps the everyday "one" from having the courage or the heart (*Mut*) to approach or confront (*aufkommen*) this anxiety before death. A frightened escape makes one misrecognize the type of nonempirical certainty that guarantees one from death. *Dasein*, then, takes refuge in gossip (*Gerede*), in tranquillization, in dissimulation, in avoiding demise, and in the race toward the anonymity of "one dies," far from the *Unheimlichkeit*—indeed, all these are structural and not accidental modalities of the *Verfallen*. The values of certainty and truth are essential for this analysis. Without being able to get into it here, let us just note that the certainty of death is described as heterogeneous to any other certainty (apodictic, theoretical, or empirical, that is to say, derived or induced—for example, from the spectacle of the other's demise). As for inauthentic existence, which evades the proper possibility of death, Heidegger defines it as untruth (*Unwahrheit*), both in this context and in others (§§44, 222). When one speaks of dying, everything thus happens at the limits of truth and untruth. In order to approach this limit further, we must move to the second series of statements, which we described above as the aporetic supplement of the first series.

This second series is an aporetic supplement because it is in the same sentence, in the interrupted unity of the same propositional

syntax in a way, that the impossibility adds an impossible complement, a complement of impossibility to possibility. Insofar as it is
its most proper possibility, and precisely as such, death is also for
*Dasein*, Heidegger ultimately says, the possibility of an impossibility. There are several modalized occurrences of this nuclear
proposition. It is often cited. However, its gripping paradox is
hardly noted, and the importance of all the successive explosions
that it holds in reserve, in the underground of the existential
analysis, is probably not measured. It is best to cite several of these
occurrences. They will force us to ask ourselves the following
questions: Is this an aporia? Where do we situate it? In the impossibility or in the possibility of an impossibility (which is not
necessarily the same thing)? What can the possibility of an impossibility be? How can we *think* that? How can we *say* it while
respecting logic and meaning? How can we approach that, live, or
*exist* it? How does one *testify* to it?

The first occurrence immediately follows the allusion to the
*s'attendre*, to the imminence of the *bevorstehen*, by which *Dasein*
stands before death [*s'attend à*] as its most proper possibility: "This
is a possibility in which," Heidegger abruptly adds, "the issue is
nothing less than Dasein's being-in-the-world [*in-der-Welt-Sein*].
Its death is the possibility of being-able-no-longer-to-be-there [*die
Möglichkeit des Nicht-mehr-dasein-könnens*]" (p. 250). Heidegger
does not say "the possibility of no longer being able to be *Dasein*"
but "the possibility of being able no longer to be there" or "of no
longer being able to be there." This is indeed the possibility of a
being-able-not-to or of a no-longer-being-able-to, but by no means
the impossibility of a being-able-to. The nuance is thin, but its very
fragility is what seems to me both decisive and significant, and it
probably is most essential in Heidegger's view. Death, the most
proper possibility of *Dasein*, is the possibility of a being-able-no-
longer-to-be-there or of a no-longer-being-able-to-be there as *Dasein*. And of that *Dasein* is absolutely certain; it can testify to it as to
a unique truth that is not comparable to any other. *Dasein* can
escape from this truth inauthentically (improperly) or approach it
authentically, properly awaiting it [*s'y attendant*] in anxiety and in

freedom. Awaiting it, that is to say, expecting and waiting for death [*s'attendant à la mort*] and waiting for itself there [*s'y attendant lui-même*]. As Heidegger adds: "As potentiality-for-being, *Dasein* cannot outstrip the possibility of death. Death is the possibility of the absolute impossibility of Dasein" (§50, p. 250).

Although I cannot do it here, it would be necessary to reconstitute a number of steps taken by Heidegger, particularly the one that concerns the modes of waiting or of anticipating and the "not yet" [*pas encore*] that are proper to *Dasein*. From an ontological point of view, this "not yet" is not the anticipation of a completion or accomplishment. It must be distinguished from what Heidegger calls the *Ausstehen* of the *Ausstand*, a term that is very difficult to translate: it partakes at the same time of the "delay," the remainder (*Rest*), which indeed is an example of it, the "remaining in waiting" (*restant en attente*, Vezin's translation), the "excess" (*excédent*, Martineau's translation), and the "still outstanding" (Macquarrie and Robinson). This "remaining," this "lack as remaining" (*das Fehlen als Ausstand*), remains, in sum, to be lived, like the piece of a set with which it is homogeneous, the part that is still absent from a whole to be completed, a "sum" in sum. By this token, and insofar as it still belongs to *Zuhandenheit*, what one can wait for, count on, expect as a remainder to be lived, is of a wholly other order than the "not yet" of *Dasein*. In the "not yet" that bends us toward death, the expecting and waiting [*le s'attendre*] is absolutely incalculable; it is without measure, and out of proportion with the time of what is left for us to live. One no longer reckons with this "not yet," and the sigh that it calls forth does not bespeak the measurable but instead the nonmeasurable: whether it lasts a second or a century, how short will life have been. Through an entirely interior path, which Heidegger does not signal, one then necessarily passes from the ontological "not yet" (*Noch-nicht*), insofar as it says what is, in the indicative, to the "not yet" of prayer and of desire, the murmured exclamation, the subjunctivity of the sigh: that death not come, *not yet!*

After these steps, Heidegger repeats two more times the proposition that I just cited. He does so according to a different linkage, indeed, but without ever lending the least attention or the least thematic interest to the logical form of the contradiction or to what goes against meaning or common sense. In the persistence of this apparently logical contradiction (the most proper possibility as the possibility of an impossibility), he even seems to see a condition of the truth, the *condition of truth*, its very unveiling, where truth is no longer measured in terms of the logical form of judgment.

Before Heidegger repeats that death is *the most proper* possibility of Dasein (*eigenste* is underlined and the expression *die eigenste Möglichkeit* opens, in a slightly liturgical tone, a whole series of paragraphs in subchapter 53, which is devoted, as its title indicates, to the authentic [*eigentliche*] being-toward-death [*Sein zum Tode*]), he emphasizes: "The closest closeness [*die nächste Nähe*] that one may have in being toward death as a possibility, is as far as possible [*so fern als möglich*] from anything actual [*einem Wirklichen*]" (§53, p. 262).

This absolute proximity is the most proper property. But since it is also as far away as possible (*so fern als möglich*), and far from any actual reality, it is the possibility of an impossible, of a nonreal as impossible. Now, in the following sentence the figure of unveiling, that is, the *truth* of this syntax, makes the impossible be, in the genitive form, the complement of the noun or the aporetic supplement of the possible (possibility *of* the impossible), but also the manifestation of the possible *as* impossible, the "as" (*als*) becoming the enigmatic figure of this monstrous coupling:

> The more unveiledly this possibility gets understood [*Je unverhüllter diese Möglichkeit verstanden wird*], the more purely [*um so reiner*] does the understanding penetrate into it [advances into, *dringt vor*] *as the possibility of the impossibility of any existence at all* [underlined by Heidegger: *als die der Unmöglichkeit der Existenz überhaupt*].

The *als* means that the possibility is both unveiled and penetrated *as* impossibility. It is not only the paradoxical possibility of a possibility of impossibility: it is possibility *as* impossibility. What is thus both unveiled (*unverhüllte*) and unveiled by, for, and during a penetrating advance (*vordringen*), is this possibility *as* impossibility, this death as the most proper possibility of *Dasein* considered as its proper impossibility. The singular motion thus named, the penetrating advance, gives or pre-gives access to the meaning of dying. Thanks to it, *Dasein* is as if in accord with (*Verstehen*) its own death. This death is both its *most proper* possibility and this same (most proper) possibility as impossibility (hence, *the least proper*, I would say, but Heidegger never says it like that). The *als* (as, considered as) keeps in reserve the most unthinkable but it is not yet the *als solche* (as such): we will have to ask ourselves how a (most proper) possibility as impossibility can still appear *as such* without immediately disappearing, without the "as such" already sinking beforehand and without its essential disappearance making *Dasein* lose everything that distinguished it—both from other forms of entities and even from the living animal in general, from the animal [*bête*]. And without its *properly-dying* being originarily contaminated and parasited by the *perishing* and the *demising*.

For the moment, let us note that the *als* is translated or relayed by the genitive form of a complement of the noun. The text imperceptibly moves from the possibility *as possibility of* the impossibility to the simple possibility *of* impossibility.

There are at least two examples:

1. "Death, as possibility, gives *Dasein* nothing to be 'actualized' [*nichts zu "Verwirklichendes"*], nothing that Dasein, considered as something actual, could *be*. It [Death] is the possibility of the impossibility [*die Möglichkeit der Unmöglichkeit*] of every way of . . . existing" (p. 262).

2. And further: "In the anticipation of this possibility [in the anticipatory precursiveness, in the *tending oneself toward* (se-tendre-vers) of the *awaiting* (s'attendre), in some way, *im Vorlaufen*], it becomes 'greater and greater' [*"immer großer"* in quotation marks; this is a strange notation: how can the possibility of death always grow greater, and what is here the measure? but the answer is probably precisely the without measure, the incalculable non-measure of truth against which this measure is measured], that is to say, the possibility reveals itself [*sich enthüllt*] as such, it reveals

itself to be such that it knows no measure at all, no more or less, but signifies the possibility of the measureless impossibility of existence [*die Möglichkeit der maßlosen Unmöglichkeit der Existenz*]" (p. 262). Further in the text (p. 265), reversing the order of presentation, Heidegger wonders how the simple impossibility of existence becomes possible, when the moment where this impossibility becomes possible remains both *absolutely certain* and *absolutely indeterminate.*

The end is approaching. Precipitation and prematuration make the law, even when the thing lasts too long. We must therefore interrupt, unjustly and arbitrarily, the patient and interminable reading that would still be required of *Being and Time* and of so many other texts, and we will rush without waiting toward some questions in the form of a provisional conclusion or of suggestions for discussion.

There are several ways of thinking the possibility of impossibility *as aporia.* Heidegger would certainly not accept making of *this* possibility of impossibility, that is, of dying, or of what I have called the "awaiting death" [*le s'attendre à la mort*], one example among others, one of these cases in which a strange logical figure of contradiction would take the form of an antinomy or of an aporia, of a problem of language or of logic to be resolved. Death—to be expected [*à laquelle s'attendre*]—is the unique occurrence of this possibility of impossibility. For it concerns the impossibility of existence itself, and not merely the impossibility of this or that. Any other determined possibility or impossibility would take on meaning and would be defined within its limits in terms of this particular possibility of impossibility, *this* particular impossibility.

While taking into consideration this absolute uniqueness, from which every uniqueness is defined, particularly every *Jemeinigkeit* of *expecting death* [*du s'attendre à la mort*], one can nevertheless retain the dynamic aspect of this question. Indeed, why not invoke the same exceptionality for the aporia of which we are speaking here (which is not just a language or logic game and which should not be classified as such too quickly)? Can one not also ask: What is the place of this unique aporia in such an "expecting death" as "expecting" the only possibility of the impossible? Is the place of this nonpassage impossibility itself or the *possibility of* impossibility? Or is it that the impossible be possible? Is the aporia the impossible itself? Indeed, the aporia is said to be impossibility, impracticability, or nonpassage: here dying would be the aporia, the impossibility of being dead, the impossibility of living or rather "existing" one's death, as well as the impossibility of existing once one is dead, or, in Heidegger's terms, the impossibility for *Dasein* to be what it is, there where it is, there, *Dasein.* Or else, on the contrary (and is it the contrary?), is this aporia the fact that the impossibility would be possible and would appear *as such*, as impossible, as an impossibility that can nevertheless appear or announce itself *as such*, an impossibility whose appearing as such would be possible (to *Dasein* and not to the living animal), an impossibility that one can await or expect, an impossibility the limits of which one can expect or at whose limits one can wait [*aux limites de laquelle on peut s'attendre*], these limits of the *as such* being, as we have seen, the limits of truth, but also of the possibility of truth? Truth and nontruth would be inseparable, and this couple would only be possible for *Dasein.* According to Heidegger, there is no nontruth for the animal, just as there is no death and no language. Truth is the truth of nontruth and vice versa. Later, after *Being and Time*, many of Heidegger's statements will suggest this.

Everything thus lies in this enigma of the "as such" and of the appearing that *at once marks and erases* the three types of limits that we have described: (1) the (anthropologico-cultural) *borders*; (2) the delimitations of the *problematic closure*, and (3) the *conceptual demarcations* of this existential analysis. To mark and at the same time to erase these lines, which only happen by erasing themselves, which only succeed in erasing themselves [*n'arrivent qu'à s'effacer*], is to trace them as still possible while also introducing the very principle of their impossibility, the principle of ruin, which is also their chance and which promises the line while compromising it in parasitism [*parasitage*], grafting, and divisibility. This principle of ruin is nothing other than death: not the dying-properly but, and it is quite different, the end of the properly-dying. This end threatens and makes possible the *analysis* itself as a discourse of de-limitation, of guaranteed dissociation, of the border or the determined closure (in the double sense of de-termination, that of the logic of termination [*terma, peras, finis*], and that of the resolute decision or of resolution—let us not forget that the analysis of *Being and Time* is also the great discourse on *Entschlossenheit*).

Heidegger does not say this and he cannot say it anywhere in *Being and Time* up to its interruption, even if such an (aporetic) form of the nonsaid can always be interpreted as denied revelation, avowal, betrayal, or symptomatic transgression, and as a secret that cannot be kept and presents itself cryptically. Besides, *death* is always the name of a secret, since it signs the irreplaceable singularity. It puts forth the public name, the common name of a secret, the common name of the proper name without name. It is therefore always a shibboleth, for the manifest name of a secret is from the beginning a private name, so that language about death is nothing but the long history of a secret society, neither public nor private, semi-private, semi-public, on the border between the two; thus, also a sort of hidden religion of the *awaiting* (oneself as well as each other), with its ceremonies, cults, liturgy, or its Marranolike rituals. A universal Marrano, if one may say, beyond what may nowadays be the finished forms of Marrano culture.

Heidegger would thus say that for *Dasein* impossibility as death—the impossibility of death, the impossibility of the existence whose name is "death"—can appear as such and announce itself; it can *make itself awaited* or *let itself be awaited* [*se faire attendre ou se laisser attendre*] as possible and as such. Only *Dasein* would be capable of this aporia, only *Dasein* has a relation to death *as such*, and this relation is not dissociable from its ability to speak, the animal being deprived of both possibilities or abilities. And it is only in the act of authentic (*eigentlich*), resolute, determinate, and decided assumption by which *Dasein* would take upon itself the possibility of this impossibility that the aporia *as such* would announce itself *as such* and purely to *Dasein* as its most proper possibility, hence as the most proper essence of *Dasein*, its freedom, its ability to question, and its opening to the meaning of being.

But here we have at least the scheme of a possible/impossible question: What difference is there between the possibility of appearing as such of the possibility of an impossibility and the impossibility of appearing *as such* of the same possibility? The impossibility of existing or of *Dasein* that Heidegger speaks of under the name of "death" is the disappearance, the end, the annihilation of the *as such*, of the possibility of the relation to the phenomenon *as such* or to the phenomenon of the "*as such.*" The impossibility that is possible for *Dasein* is, indeed, that there not be or that there no longer be *Dasein*: that precisely what is possible become impossible, from then on no longer appearing as such. It is nothing less than the end of the world, with each death, each time that we expect no longer to be able to await ourselves and each other [*nous attendre*], hence no longer to be able to understand each other [*nous entendre*]. According to Heidegger, it is therefore the impossibility of the "as such" that, *as such*, would be possible to *Dasein* and not to any form of entity and living thing. But if the impossibility of the "as such" is indeed the impossibility of the "as such," it is also what cannot appear as such. Indeed, this relation to the disappearing as such of the "as such"—the "as such" that Heidegger makes the distinctive mark and the specific ability of *Dasein*—is also the characteristic common *both* to the inauthentic *and* to the authentic forms of the existence of *Dasein*, common to all experiences of death (properly dying, perishing, and demising), and also, outside of *Dasein*, common to all living things in general. Common characteristic does not mean homogeneity, but rather the impossibility of an absolutely pure and rigorously uncrossable limit (in terms of existence or of concepts) between an existential analysis of death and a fundamental anthropo-theology, and moreover between anthropological cultures of death and animal cultures of death. Against, or without, Heidegger, one could point to a thousand signs that show that animals also *die*. Although the innumerable structural differences that separate one "species" from another should make us vigilant about any discourse on animality or bestiality *in general*, one can say that animals have a very significant relation to death, to murder and to war (hence, to borders), to mourning and to hospitality, and so forth, even if they have neither a relation to death nor to the "name" of death as such, nor, by the same token, to the other as such, to the purity as such of the alterity of the other as such. But neither does man, that is precisely the point! Nor does even man as *Dasein*, assuming that one could ever rigorously say man and man as *Dasein*. Who will guarantee that the name, the ability to name death (like that of naming the other, and it is the same) does not participate as much in the dissimulation of the "as such" of death as in its revelation, and that language is not precisely the origin of the nontruth of death, and of the other?

For, conversely, if death is indeed the possibility of the impossible and therefore the possibility of appearing as such of the impossibility of appearing as such either, then man, or man as *Dasein*, never has a relation to death as such, but only to perishing, to demising, and to the death of the other, who is not the other. The death of the other thus becomes again "first," always first. It is like the experience of mourning that institutes my relation to myself and constitutes the egoity of the *ego* as well as every *Jemeinigkeit* in the *différance*—neither internal nor external—that structures this experience. The death of the other, this death of the other in "me," is fundamentally the only death that is named in the syntagm "my death," with all the consequences that one can draw from this. This is another dimension of awaiting [*s'attendre*] as awaiting one another [*s'attendre l'un l'autre*], awaiting oneself at death and expecting death [*s'attendre soi-même à la mort*] by awaiting one another [*s'attendant l'un l'autre*], up to the most advanced longevity in a life that will have been so short, no matter what.

This nonaccess to death as such—but this access only to the aspect of the border that can only be the threshold, the step, as one says of the approach to the border—is also what Heidegger calls the impossible, the access to death as nonaccess to a nonborder, as the possibility of the impossible. But one can turn what is thus at the very heart of the possibility of the existential analysis against the whole apparatus of *Being and Time*, against the very possibility of the existential analysis. When Blanchot constantly repeats[18]—and it is a long complaint and not a triumph of life—the impossible dying, the impossibility, alas, of dying, he says at once the same thing and something completely different from Heidegger. It is just a question of knowing in which sense (in the sense of direction and trajectory) one reads the expression the possibility of impossibility.

If death, the most proper possibility of *Dasein*, is the possibility of its impossibility, death becomes the most improper possibility and the most ex-propriating, the most inauthenticating one. From the most originary inside of its possibility, the proper of *Dasein* becomes from then on contaminated, parasited, and divided by the most improper. Heidegger indeed says that inauthenticity is not an exterior accident, a sin or an evil that comes by surprise to existence in its authentic mode. This is where Heidegger at least claims to dissociate *Verfallen* from the original sin and from any morality as well as from any theology. But he crucially needs the distinction between the authentic and the inauthentic, as well as that among the different forms of *ending*: *dying properly speaking*, *perishing*, and *demising*. These distinctions are threatened in their very principle, and, in truth, they remain impracticable as soon as one admits that an ultimate possibility is nothing other than the possibility of an impossibility and that the *Enteignis* always inhabited *Eigentlichkeit* before even being named there—indeed, this will happen later.

To that which lives without having a name, we will give an added name: Marrano, for example. Playing with the relative arbitrariness of every nomination, we determine this added name [*surnom*], which a name always is, in memory of and according to the figure of the Marrano (of the crypto-judaic, and of the crypto-X in general). As we suggested just a while ago, it is said that the history of the Marranos has just come to an end with the declaration by the Spanish court [in 1992]. You can believe that if you want to.

We will not deploy this aporetic "logic" much longer. The principle of all the consequences that one can draw from it is fearsome. For what guarantees its ultimate resource to the existential analysis of *Dasein* (that is, the "as such" of death) is also what ruins the very possibility of the analysis from within. It therefore compromises all at once: (1) the phenomenological principle of the "as such" that regulates its method; (2) the problematic closures that the analysis draws in its relation to other disciplines; and (3) the conceptual limits that the analysis puts into operation: for example, the limits between *Dasein* and the being of other entities (*Vorhandensein, Zuhandensein*) or other living things, between the speaking being that has a world and the animal "poor of world" (*weltarm*) (this makes all the difference in the world, it concerns all the borders of the world); but also the limits between ending and perishing (*enden/ verenden*), dying and perishing (*sterben/ verenden*), dying and demising (*sterben/ ableben*).

In the French idiom, we could add the distinction among: (1) to be *oneself* awaiting [*s'attendre soi-même*] (death) in an always too short life; (2) to be expecting death and *that* death come [*s'attendre à la mort et que la mort vienne*] (always too soon or too late, untimely); and (3) to be waiting for each other, waiting for/in death as for/at the limits of truth [*s'attendre l'un l'autre à la mort comme aux limites de la vérité*].

What appears to be refused is the pure possibility of cutting off. Among *border, closure*, and *demarcation*, who would be able to cut this braid in which I have let myself be taken and that I am going to leave here? Leaving it open or fraying it at each of its ends, let us describe the three twisting movements that keep it open and ultimately interminable, in other words *without end.*

*First*, it involves the aporia, since that was my theme. What we have glimpsed, I hope, and the lesson that I draw for the usage I was able or may be able from now on to make of the aporia, is that if one must endure the aporia, if such is the law of all decisions, of all responsibilities, of all duties without duty, and of all the border problems that ever can arise, *the aporia can never simply be endured as such.* The ultimate aporia is the impossibility of the aporia *as such*. The reservoir of this statement seems to me incalculable. This statement is made with and reckons with the incalculable itself. Death, as the possibility of the impossible *as such*, is a figure of the aporia in which "death" and death can replace—and this is a metonymy that carries the name beyond the name and beyond the name of name—all that is only possible as impossible, if there is such a thing: love, the gift, the other, testimony, and so forth.

*Second*, it involves what from the beginning foils every methodological strategy and every stratagem of delimitation. Circumscription is the impossible. I hope that I have convinced you my purpose was not to justify a passage beyond knowledge, anthropothanatology, biology, or the metaphysics of death toward a more radical, originary, or fundamental thought, as if the limit were a known edge between, on the one hand, anthropology (be it even a fundamental anthropology) and, on the other hand, ontology, an existential analysis, and more generally a more questioning thought of death in general. On the contrary, based on the example of Heidegger or of the virtual debate among Heidegger, Levinas, and Freud, my discourse was aimed at suggesting that this fundamentalist dimension is untenable and that it cannot even claim to have any coherence or rigorous specificity. It remains untenable, even if one thinks in an original way the limits of this coherence or of this specificity in the form of a system, of the unity of a field, or of an archi-region, etc. While the richest or most necessary anthropo-thanatology cannot found itself in any other way than on presuppositions that do not belong to its knowledge or its competence, and while these presuppositions therefore constitute a style of questioning of which Heidegger, Freud, and Levinas are remarkable witnesses, conversely this fundamental questioning cannot protect itself from a hidden bio-anthropo-thanato-theological contamination.

*Finally*, since this contaminating contraband remains irreducible, it already insinuates itself through the idiom of the existential analysis. One will always be able to consider the existential analysis as a *witness*—and I keep for this term *witness* the ambiguity by which, as you may remember, we characterized the clause of belonging without belonging that is the condition of any testimony, and of its language first of all. What is analysis witness to? Well, precisely to that from which it demarcates itself, here mainly from the culture characterized by the so-called religions of the Book. Despite all the distance taken from anthropo-theology, indeed, from Christian onto-theology, the analysis of death in *Being and Time* nonetheless repeats all the essential motifs of such onto-theology, a repetition that bores into its originarity right down to its ontological foundation, whether it concerns the fall, the *Verfallen*, into the inauthenticity of relaxation or distraction, or the *sollicitudo*, the *cura*, and the care (*Sorge*), or sin and originary guilt (*Schuldigsein*), or anxiety, and, regarding the texts, whether it concerns St. Augustine, Meister Eckhart, Pascal, Kierkegaard, or a few others. Whatever the enigma of this repetition, as well as of the concept of repetition deployed by Heidegger, I'll just say, without being able to go into it in any depth, that neither the language nor the process of this analysis of death is possible without the Christian experience, indeed, the Judeo-Christiano-Islamic experience of death to which the analysis testifies. Without this event and the irreducible historicity to which it testifies. The same could be said for Freud's and Levinas's thought, *mutatis mutandis.* Considering what we just have seen concerning borders, demarcations, and limits, the only characteristic that we can stress here is that of an irreducibly double inclusion: the including and the included regularly exchange places in this strange topography of edges. Instead of deploying the concept at length, I will simply point to the example.

*On the one hand,* no matter how rich or new it may be, one can read a history of death in the Christian West, like that of Ariès for example, as a small monograph that illustrates like a footnote the extent to which it relies, in its presuppositions, upon the powerful and universal delimitation that the existential analysis of death in *Being and Time* is. The existential analysis exceeds and therefore includes beforehand the work of the historian, not to mention the biologist, the psychologist, and the theologian of death. It also conditions their work; it is constantly presupposed there.

However, *on the other hand,* conversely but just as legitimately, one can also be tempted to read *Being and Time* as a small, late document, among many others *within* the huge archive where the memory of death in Christian Europe is being accumulated. Each of these two discourses on death is much more comprehensive than the other, bigger and smaller than what it tends to include or exclude, more and less originary, more and less ancient, young or old.

Maybe we have the age, an age among others, of this anachronism.

How can one have an age among others? How does one calculate the age of a Marrano, for example?

Let us figuratively call Marrano anyone who remains faithful to a secret that he has not chosen, in the very place where he lives, in the home of the inhabitant or of the occupant, in the home of the first or of the second *arrivant,* in the very place where he stays without saying no but without identifying himself as belonging to. In the unchallenged night where the radical absence of any historical witness keeps him or her, in the dominant culture that by definition has calendars, this secret keeps the Marrano even before the Marrano keeps it. Is it not possible to think that such a secret eludes history, age, and aging?

Thanks to this anachronism, Marranos that we are, Marranos in any case, whether we want to be or not, whether we know it or not, Marranos having an incalculable number of ages, hours, and years, of untimely histories, each both larger and smaller than the other, each still waiting for the other, we may incessantly be younger and older, in a last word, infinitely finished.

# Notes

1. The "paternity" here is that of Denis Diderot, and the "limits of truth" he bespeaks in his *Essai sur la vie de Sénèque le philosophe, sur ses écrits, et sur les règnes de Claude et de Néron*, in vol. 7 of *Oeuvres de Sénèque traduites en français par feu M. Lagrange* (Paris: Frères de Bure, 1778). Diderot's essay was published in 1782 in a second edition with the title *Essai sur les règnes de Claude et de Néron et sur les moeurs et les écrits de Sénèque, pour servir d'introduction à la lecture de ce philosophe*, to be found in *Diderot: Oeuvres complètes* (Paris: Herman, 1986): 25: 363–71. Unless otherwise identified, all translations below are my own.—Trans.

2. Seneca, "On the Shortness of Life," in vol. 2 of *Moral Essays*, trans. John W. Basore (Cambridge: Harvard University Press, 1932): Book 10: 3.1–4 (translation modified).

3. Ibid. 10: 3.5–4.2.

4. Cicero, *De finibus bonorum et malorum*, ed. Thomas Schiche (Stuttgart: B. G. Teubner, 1961).

5. Sophocles, *Oedipus the King*, trans. David Grene in *Sophocles I* (Chicago: University of Chicago Press, 1973): ll. 1528–30.

6. Jacques Derrida, *Margins of Philosophy*, trans. Alan Bass (Chicago: University of Chicago Press, 1982), p. 39.

7. In this and the following paragraph, the author mentions these works of his (English translations have been listed where they exist): "Tympan," in ibid.; *Glas*, trans. John P. Leavey, Jr., and Richard Rand (Lincoln: University of Nebraska Press, 1986); "Fors: The Anglish Words of Nicolas Abraham and Maria Torok," trans. Barbara Johnson, *The Georgia Review* (Spring 1977), pp. 64–116; *Mémoires for Paul de Man*,

83

trans. Cecile Lindsay, Jonathan Culler, and Eduardo Cadava (New York: Columbia University Press, 1986); *Psyché: Inventions de l'autre* (Paris: Editions Galilée, 1987); *Parages* (Paris: Editions Galilée, 1986); *Schibboleth: Pour Paul Celan* (Paris: Editions Galilée, 1986); *Limited Inc.*, re-edited, with "Toward an Ethic of Discussion" (Evanston: Northwestern University Press, 1988); *Du droit à la philosophie* (Paris: Editions Galilée, 1990); *Donner le temps, 1: La fausse monnaie* (Paris: Editions Galilée, 1991), in English as *Given Time, 1. Counterfeit Money*, trans. Peggy Kamuf (Chicago: University of Chicago Press, 1992); *The Other Heading*, trans. Pascale-Anne Brault and Michael B. Naas (Bloomington: Indiana University Press, 1992); "Passions," in *Derrida: A Critical Reader*, ed. David Wood (Oxford: Basil Blackwell, 1992); "Donner la mort," in *L'Ethique du don*, ed. Jean-Michel Rabaté and Michael Wetzel (Paris: Transition, 1992).—Trans.

8. *The Other Heading*, pp. 76–78.

9. Ibid., pp. 80–81.

10. Indeed, what Kant calls the *peace alliance* (*foedus pacificum*), which is distinct from the *peace contract* (*pactum pacis*), links the States in order to end all wars. Always involving state control, interstate and therefore intrastate control, this alliance aims not at political power but at assuring the freedom of the State as such, of one of the States and of the States that are its allies. This idea of federation "should progressively spread to all States and thus lead to perpetual peace." In Kant's view, this is the only rational means for leaving war and the savage, lawless state behind. Thus, it would be a matter of constituting a "*State of peoples* (actually growing ceaselessly), which will finally gather all the peoples of the earth." But since the peoples do not want such a State, "only the negative equivalent of a permanent alliance, protecting against war and always extending itself further, can, in the place of the positive idea of a *world republic* (if one does not want to lose everything), hold back the warring inclination that fears law but that presents the constant danger of exploding" (*Zum ewigen Frieden*). The themes of this conference would demand of us that we reflect and also transpose what, according to Kant, follows from these cosmopolitan rights with respect to *hospitality* and the *secret.* (1) The *hospitalitas* should give the foreigner the right not to be treated as an enemy when he arrives on the other's territory. But if one has the right to send the foreigner back, it is on the condition that this expulsion not rush him toward his ruin. And for as long as he "stays quietly in his place," one should not treat him as an enemy. But if the

foreigner only has, to be sure, the *right to visit* and not that of *residence*, this right to visit is to be extended to all mankind. Why? Because this right is based upon the "right of the communal possession of the surface of the earth." The earth being spherical, infinite dispersion is excluded as a possibility. No one has originally more right to occupy territory than anyone else, and people must indeed live alongside one another. (2) Concerning the secret, that is, a sort of shibboleth in legal relations [*relations de droit*], doesn't it occupy here a very unique place? Certainly public law [*droit public*] excludes the secret from its *content*, as an *objective* contradiction of terms. But "subjectively" the author of an article can want to keep the secret and judge that it is a matter of his dignity. Concerning international relations, there is only one secret in view of perpetual peace (*Geheimer Artikel zum ewigen Frieden*): "The States armed for war should consult the maxims of the philosophers concerning the conditions of public peace." If the legislator of a State seems to discredit himself by seeking instruction from those citizens who the philosophers are, when it concerns relations with other States, he is nonetheless "advised" to do it, Kant says. But he should do it "tacitly" (*stillschweigend*; i.e., by making a secret [*Geheimnis*] of it); he is advised to let the philosophers speak freely and publicly of universal maxims about war and peace. Not that the State should prefer philosophical principles to the sentences of the jurist who represents the power of the State, but the State should *listen to* the philosopher. This is the logic of the *Conflict of Faculties*: "The faculty of philosophy, subjected to these united powers, finds itself at a very low level. . . . One must not expect that kings philosophize or that philosophers become kings, but one must also not wish for it because holding power inevitably corrupts the free judgment of reason. But it is indispensable to the clarification of power's affairs that kings and royalty (controlling themselves by following the laws of egality) do not let the class of philosophers disappear or be deprived of speech, but instead let it speak publicly, and, because the class of philosophers, by its nature, is incapable of unifying itself into bands or clubs, it cannot be suspected, by any scandalmongering, of *propaganda* [*Propagande*]." This place granted to the secret in the practice of politics, in legislative activity, and in the conduct of international affairs escapes from public law and public space, as well as from publicity and from the *res publica* of the State, a zone of the *socius* that, although not public, is not private either, and, although not belonging to law, does not stem from reality or from natural savagery either. Before all these oppositions or fundamental distinctions, before all these critical delimitations, the secret possibility of the secret seems to situate, in truth to prescribe, the very place of the philosophers' deliberate (premeditated) intervention in the juridico-political space. One would have to draw all the consequences. But they remain incalculable, incalculably dangerous in what they promise or in what they threaten: concerning the secret of politics, the politics of the secret, and first of all the concept of the secret put here into operation.

11. Martin Heidegger, *Sein und Zeit*, 16th ed. (Tübingen: Max Niemeyer, 1986); *Being and Time*, trans. John Macquarrie and Edward Robinson (New York: Harper, 1962). Page numbers refer to the German edition and are given in the margins of the English translation. The English translation has occasionally been modified to coincide with the French translation used by the author.—Trans.

12. Vezin was the first French translator of *Sein und Zeit* (*Etre et Temps*, Paris: Gallimard, 1986); Martineau's translation appeared as *Etre et temps* from Authentica in 1985.—Trans.

13. *Arrivant* can mean "arrival," "newcomer," or "arriving."—Trans.

14. After the fact, I remembered the *arrivant* of *La*, the book by Hélène Cixous (Paris: Gallimard, 1976; Paris: Editions des Femmes, 1979), p. 132, and the play that she presented in 1977 in Avignon, precisely under the title of *L'Arrivante*.

15. Martin Heidegger, *Unterwegs zur Sprache* (Pfullingen: Günther Neske, 1959): p. 215; *On the Way to Language*, trans. Peter D. Hertz (New York: Harper, 1971): p. 107.

16. Emmanuel Levinas, "La Mort et le temps," *Cours de 1975–76* in *L'Herne* 60 (Paris: Editions de l'Herne, 1991): p. 38.

17. It is appropriate to cite Sade's will here, a will that leaves to a certain Le Normand both Sade's body and the ceremony of its burial in a certain château: "Finally, a last case—both utopic for the eighteenth century and already anachronistic for the year 1806—is the will written with seriousness and conviction by the Divine Marquis. It testifies to a complete confusion of the two similar but separate opinions, the disregard for the body and the radical refusal of immortality. Sade requests that just after his death 'an express letter be sent to Sir Le Normand, wood merchant . . . in order to request that he come himself, accompanied by a cart, to pick up my body so as to transport it under his escort in the said cart to the woods of my property in Malmaison . . . near Epernon, where I want it to be placed without any ceremony in the first

thick copse that is to be found in the said woods off to the right when you enter them from the side of the former castle by the large path that separates it. The grave made in the copse will be dug by the farmer of Malmaison under the inspection of Sir Le Normand, who shall not leave my body until after having placed it in the said grave. He may be accompanied in this ceremony, if he wishes so, by those of my parents or friends who, without any sort of pomp, will be so kind as to give me this mark of attachment. Once the grave is covered, it shall be *covered by acorns strewn over it* so that, in time, the terrain of the said grave being once again replenished and the copse being thickened as it was before, the traces of my tomb disappear from the surface of the earth, as I flatter myself that my memory will be effaced from the spirit of mankind [it is pure vanity to want to impose it with a monument], except nonetheless the small number of those who have been so kind as to love me up to the last moment and of whom I take a very sweet memory to the tomb,'" Philippe Ariès, *L'Homme devant la mort*, 2: 61–62. The bracketed remark, one will have understood, is Ariès's, who concludes his chapter in this way: "The utopian will of the Marquis de Sade indicates a slant of the epoch, a slant that was never to be descended all the way to the bottom, but which attracted even the Christians and gave to a part of society the vertigo of nothingness."

18.  See in particular *L'Attente l'oubli* (1962), *Le pas au-delà* (1973); *The Step Not Beyond*, trans. Lycette Nelson (Albany: State University of New York Press, 1990); and *L'Écriture du désastre* (1980); *The Writing of the Disaster*, trans. Ann Smock (Lincoln: University of Nebraska Press, 1986). It would now be necessary to re-read and cite these texts from beginning to end. Not able to do that here, I refer at least, in a much too insufficient way, to the pages of the last book, pages that begin "Dying means: you are dead already, in an immemorial past, of a death which was not yours. . . . This uncertain death, always anterior—this vestige of a past that never has been present—is never individual. . . . Impossible necessary death . . . one lives and speaks only by killing the *infans* in oneself (in others also); but what is the infans?" (*Writing*, pp. 65–67). Here as elsewhere one can recognize the reference to Heidegger, notably to the thinking of death as "the possibility of impossibility" (*Writing*, p. 70). The apparent neutrality of this reference (neither an approbation nor a critique) deserves a patient and original treatment that we cannot undertake here.

# MERIDIAN

*Crossing Aesthetics*

Library of Congress
Cataloging-in-Publication Data

Derrida, Jacques,
[Apories, English]
Aporias : dying—awaiting (one another at)
the "limits of truth"
(mourir—s'attendre aux "limites
de la vérité") / Jacques Derrida ;
translated by Thomas Dutoit.
p.  cm. — (Meridian)
Includes bibliographical references.
ISBN 0–8047–2233–1 (alk. paper) —
ISBN 0–8047–2252–8 (pbk. : alk. paper)
1. Death.   2. Contradiction.
3. Belief and doubt.  I. Title.
II. Series: Meridian
(Stanford, Calif.)
BD444.D46513   1993
128'.5—dc20
93–29865
CIP

♾ This book is printed on acid-free paper.
It was typeset in Adobe Garamond and
Lithos by Keystone Typesetting, Inc.